DUE DATE

DEC 1 4 1999	MAR 0 8 2005	
DEC - 1 1999		
DEC 06 2001		
MAR 2 8 2002		
APR 0 2 2002		
APR 0 1 2003		
APR 0 1 2003		
MAY 2 0 2005		
201-6503		Printed in USA

Airline Passenger Security Screening

New Technologies
and Implementation Issues

Committee on Commercial Aviation Security

Panel on Passenger Screening

National Materials Advisory Board

Commission on Engineering and Technical Systems

National Research Council

Publication NMAB–482–1
National Academy Press
Washington, D.C. 1996

The study by the National Materials Advisory Board was conducted under Contract No. DTFA03-94-C-00068 with the Federal Aviation Administration.

Library of Congress Catalog Card Number 96-69048
International Standard Book Number ISBN-0-309-05439-7

PANEL ON PASSENGER SCREENING

GEORGE SWENSON, JR. (chair), University of Illinois, Champaign
HOMER BOYNTON, consultant, Hilton Head Island, South Carolina
BARRY D. CRANE, Institute for Defense Analyses, Alexandria, Virginia
DOUGLAS H. HARRIS, Anacapa Sciences, Inc., Charlottesville, Virginia
WILFRED (BILL) JACKSON, University of North Dakota, Grand Forks
JIRI (ART) JINATA, Pacific Northwest National Laboratory, Richland, Washington
KENNETH R. LAUGHERY, Rice University, Houston, Texas
HARRY E. MARTZ, Lawrence Livermore National Laboratory, Livermore, California
KENNETH MOSSMAN, Arizona State University, Scottsdale
PAUL ROTHSTEIN, Georgetown University, Washington, D.C.

National Materials Advisory Board Liaison Representative

JAMES WAGNER, The Johns Hopkins University, Baltimore, Maryland

National Materials Advisory Board Staff

SANDRA HYLAND, senior program manager
JANICE M. PRISCO, project assistant

Acknowledgments

The Panel on Passenger Screening would like to acknowledge the contributions of the many individuals who contributed to this study, including meeting speakers and the organizational representatives who attended the workshop held by the panel. The panel is particularly grateful to those who submitted statements to the panel after the workshop to ensure that the points they raised were included in this report. For his overview of technologies that might be considered for screening airline passengers, we also thank Lyle Malotky, Scientific Advisor to the FAA Associate Administrator for Civil Aviation Security.

Extensive background research and writing on the legal aspects of passenger screening technologies and the introduction of other new surveillance technologies was performed by Thaddeus Pope. The panel thanks Mr. Pope for his efforts.

The panel is grateful for the contributions of the two FAA contracting office technical representatives, Ron Krauss and Jim Connelly, of the Aviation Research and Development Division at the FAA Technical Center. The panel also acknowledges the support from Program Director Paul Polski.

The panel wishes to thank Janice Prisco, Jack Hughes, and Sandra Hyland of the National Materials Advisory Board for their help in editing and preparing this report.

Preface

The Federal Aviation Administration (FAA) requested the National Research Council (NRC) to prepare a report assessing issues concerning the implementation of new, automated passenger screening methods and barriers to their implementation. The Panel on Passenger Screening was established by the NRC for this purpose. These automated methods are used to detect concealed weapons and explosives being carried by people. The FAA supports the development of promising passenger screening technologies capable of detecting not only metal-based weapons (as current screening technologies are able to do), but also plastic explosives and other non-metallic threat materials and objects. However, the FAA is concerned that these new technologies may not be appropriate for implementation, for reasons other than technical performance. Therefore, the FAA asked panel members to primarily focus on aspects of the new passenger screening technologies that could cause apprehension among passengers.

The panel was formed by the National Materials Advisory Board of the NRC to (1) review all potential automated instrumental methods currently under consideration for passenger screening applications, (2) assess aspects of each method that could cause concerns over health risks (e.g., exposure to radiation), privacy, and traveler comfort, in light of current and anticipated health regulations, privacy laws, and public concerns, (3) consider ways in which the methods could be implemented to maintain high levels of effectiveness, while minimizing health risks and increasing public acceptance, (4) determine the key factors that could affect airport implementation and suggest mitigating strategies, (5) suggest alternate screening methods for passengers who wish to avoid the automated system, and (6) assess mechanisms for clearing alarms.

The panel met five times between February and September 1995. Two of the meetings focused on obtaining information on current and prospective passenger screening technologies and on passenger screening procedures in other countries. During one of these two meetings, panel members visited a major airport for a detailed inspection of screening facilities and methods. The panel also hosted a workshop attended by representatives of a number of organizations concerned with air carrier operations, airport operations, and passenger privacy. The workshop participants shared their views about the new technologies and their potential concerns about implementing these technologies in airports.

In addressing the formal task statement, the panel determined that the effectiveness of both current and future aviation security systems depends strongly on the human elements of the system. Therefore, the panel included and addressed two issues not specified in the formal task statement: (1) how existing systems can be made more effective without the addition of completely new technologies, and (2) whether greater attention should be given to "human factors," including the use of passenger profiling techniques. This report is the result of the panel deliberations.

George W. Swenson, Jr., Chair

Contents

EXECUTIVE SUMMARY 1

1 INTRODUCTION 6
  Development of Aviation Security, 6
  Passenger Screening, 6
  Key Issues, 9

2 METHODOLOGY 11
  Panel Meetings, 11
  Workshop on Passenger Screening, 11
  Summary, 12

3 PASSENGER SCREENING TECHNOLOGIES 13
  Passenger-Profiling System, 13
  Imaging Technologies, 14
  Trace-Detection technologies, 16
  Nonimaging Electromagnetic Technologies, 19
  Clearing an Alarm, 20
  Summary, 21

4 OPERATIONAL AND COST ISSUES 22
  Air Carrier Operations, 22
  Airport Facilities Operations, 22
  Delays Caused by Aviation Security Measures, 23
  Summary, 23

5 OPERATOR ERGONOMICS, SELECTION, TRAINING, AND
  MOTIVATION 24
  Relationship between Pay and Performance, 24
  Ergonomics in System Design, 25
  Operator Selection, Training, and Motivation, 26
  Measuring Operator Performance, 26
  Potential Operator Concerns with Specific Screening Technologies, 26
  Summary, 27

6 HEALTH EFFECTS 28
  Cancer, 28
  Reproductive Health Effects, 30
  Heart Disease and Pacemakers, 31
  Some Possible Health Concerns Associated with Specific Screening Technologies, 31
  Summary, 32

7 LEGAL ISSUES 34
    Unconstitutional Search, 34
    Tort Claims, 39
    Role of the FAA, 41
    Some Possible Legal Concerns Associated with Specific Screening Technologies, 41
    Summary, 42

8 PUBLIC ACCEPTANCE 44
    Public Concerns about Health Effects, 44
    Public Concerns about Privacy, 44
    Public Concerns about Convenience, 45
    Public Concerns about Comfort, 45
    Assessing Public Acceptance, 46
    Results of the Workshop on New Technologies for Passenger Screening, 46
    Some Possible Public Acceptance Concerns Associated with Specific Screening
        Technologies, 49
    Summary, 50

9 CONCLUSIONS AND RECOMMENDATIONS 52
    Assessment of System Enhancements, 52
    Improvements to Current Screening Systems, 53
    Technologies to Meet Future Passenger Screening Requirements, 53
    Operator Performance, 54

REFERENCES 57

APPENDICES
    A LAWS, REGULATIONS, AND TREATIES 63

    B FOLLOW-UP INFORMATION FROM WORKSHOP ATTENDEES 65

    C SELECTED LEGAL CASES RELEVANT TO AVIATION SECURITY 68

    D BIOGRAPHICAL SKETCHES OF PANEL MEMBERS 73

Tables and Figures

TABLES

1-1   Responsibilities of Air Carriers, Airport Operators, and the FAA for Passenger Screening, 8

2-1   Speakers and Topics Presented to the Panel on Passenger Screening, 11

2-2   Organizations at the Workshop on New Technologies for Passenger Screening, 12

3-1   Passenger Screening Technologies Based on Imaging, 14

3-2   Passenger Screening Technologies Based on Trace Detection, 19

8-1   Principal Concerns Associated with Health and Privacy, as Identified at the Workshop on New Technologies for Passenger Screening, 47

8-2   Principal Concerns Associated with Comfort and Convenience, as Identified at the Workshop on New Technologies for Passenger Screening, 48

FIGURES

1-1   Hijacking and bombing incidents aboard U.S.- and foreign-registered aircraft, 1968–1994, 7

3-1   El Al Airlines system for identifying people who could be threats, 13

3-2   The electromagnetic spectrum, 14

3-3a   Visual image of a person being scanned by the Contraband Detection System produced by Millitech, 15

3-3b   Millimeter-wave image of the same person showing two weapons hidden under the subject's sweater, 15

3-4   Person being scanned (front image) using the SECURE 1000 active x-ray imaging system produced by Nicolet Imaging Systems, 16

3-5   Image created by the SECURE 1000, produced by Nicolet Imaging Systems, showing several threat objects, including a half-pound simulated explosive charge and a .38 caliber handgun, 17

3-6a   Visual image of a person being scanned by the BodySearch 1 produced by AS&E, 18

3-6b   X-ray image of the same person showing a variety of hidden threat objects, including a Plexiglas knife, a 9mm handgun, and simulated drugs, 18

5-1   Factors that influence job performance, 25

6-1   Comparison of levels of exposure from common ionizing radiation sources, 29

Executive Summary

This study deals with issues that could arise, should the Federal Aviation Administration (FAA) mandate the implementation in airports of new passenger screening technologies that are currently available or are being developed. The objectives of this study were (1) to review all potential automated instrumental methods currently under FAA consideration for passenger screening, (2) to assess aspects of each method that could cause concerns over health risks (e.g., exposure to radiation), privacy, and traveler comfort, in light of current and anticipated health regulations, privacy laws, and public concerns, (3) to consider ways to maintain effectiveness while increasing public acceptance and minimizing health risks, (4) to determine key factors that could affect airport implementation and suggest mitigating strategies, (5) to suggest alternate screening methods for passengers who wish to avoid the automated system, and (6) assess mechanisms for clearing alarms.

BACKGROUND

Ensuring the safety of the U.S. air travel system and of American and foreign air carriers traveling to and from the United States is a monumental task. Currently, in the United States this involves screening more than 1.5 million passengers and their carry-on baggage every day for the presence of metallic weapons and other dangerous materials. To address current security requirements, the FAA is examining new technologies designed to enhance the effectiveness of existing screening procedures. At the same time, the FAA is investigating other technologies that would enable existing systems, which, at present, can detect only metallic weapons, to detect other types of dangerous objects and substances (e.g., plastic explosives). These improvements are necessary as preparation for anticipated changes in security requirements.

An ideal passenger screening technology would be capable of detecting both metallic and nonmetallic threat items in less than six seconds, with a high degree of accuracy (including a high detection rate with a low false-alarm rate). In addition, an ideal system would give the operator enough information in an appropriate format to allow for the speedy and accurate resolution of alarms.

Current passenger security-screening requirements were developed in response to an increase in hijackings prior to 1972. Passenger screening procedures in place today focus on finding passengers carrying metallic weapons that might be used to intimidate the crew into changing the destination of an aircraft. However, because of increasing international political unrest and the attractiveness of U.S. aircraft as terrorists targets, the FAA has recognized the need to improve the capabilities of existing airport security screening systems and processes. These improvements include (1) enhancing the ability of metal-detection portals to operate effectively in an electrically noisy environment, (2) providing better information to security screening personnel on the type and location of potential weapons on individuals who trigger metal-detection portal alarms, and (3) increasing the detection capabilities of existing systems by adding the ability to detect a broader spectrum of metals and alloys, plastic explosives, and other threat materials.

Trace-detection technologies, which detect the presence of explosive materials by reacting to their vapors or particles, can be used to supplement existing metal-detection technologies to build more comprehensive security systems. Metal-detection portal systems can be replaced by technologies that can produce images that reveal objects concealed under layers of clothing and that enable security personnel to identify both metallic and nonmetallic threat objects.

These potential improvements to current screening technologies, as well as new technologies that meet anticipated future screening requirements, have technical features that strengthen their detection capabilities. However, the acceptance or rejection of a technology both by the people required to use it (e.g., airport operators and air carriers) and by the people affected by it (e.g., passengers and crews) is just as important as the performance and effectiveness of the technology. Air carriers will resist the implementation of a detection technology (no matter how perfect), if it is unacceptable to the traveling public. Thus, a technology could fail for largely nontechnical reasons. The panel identified the following nontechnical issues of potential public concern in relation to new passenger screening technologies:

- *Health.* Will the technology harm or injure people? Will people perceive the technology as dangerous?

- *Legal.* (other than health-related lawsuits, subsumed in "Health" above). Do certain aspects of the technology violate the rights of individuals under the Fourth Amendment to the Constitution of the United States, which guarantees against unreasonable search and seizure? Does it violate the legal right to privacy? Will people perceive either of these possibilities to be true?
- *Operational.* Will the technology require additional space in airport terminals? Will air carriers be able to screen passengers accurately and rapidly enough to maintain flight schedules?
- *Privacy.* Even if not a legally cognizable invasion of privacy, will the technology make people feel as though their privacy is being invaded? Will the screening process reveal personal information that passengers would rather keep to themselves?
- *Convenience.* Will passengers be able to proceed quickly through the system and to their gates? Will the new technology take more time to screen passengers than current procedures?

To examine these issues, the panel conducted three information-gathering meetings, including a workshop on new technologies for passenger screening. The workshop was attended by representatives of air carriers, airport operators, specialists in aviation security screening systems in other countries, and individuals interested in the legal aspects of passenger screening. With input from this wide variety of sources, panel members were able to address the five nontechnical issues listed above, along with other questions that emerged in the course of the study.

The major conclusions of the panel are as follows:

- The level of discomfort, inconvenience, cost, and personal intrusion air carriers and travelers are willing to tolerate is strongly influenced by their perceptions of the severity of the threat, the urgency of the situation, and the effectiveness of the efforts to deter the threat.
- Even without adding more advanced screening equipment, current screening systems and procedures can be improved significantly by placing greater emphasis on human factors.

The panel makes the following general recommendations to aid the FAA for determining which new technologies are appropriate for passenger screening:

- Emphasize the link between the invasiveness and inconvenience of the screening technology and the threat being addressed in a strategy for implementing new passenger screening technologies.
- Emphasize programs that improve the effectiveness of the operator as a part the security system.

LINKS BETWEEN PASSENGER INCONVENIENCE AND LEVEL OF THREAT

The panel determined that air carriers and the traveling public relate the extent of passenger screening they consider acceptable and adequate to the severity of the threat they believe is being averted by the screening process. For example, air carriers and passengers accept the more intensive security procedures used for international flights because they perceive a higher likelihood of terrorists targeting international flights. Passengers would probably resent the application of similarly tight security measures to domestic flights, unless authorities could prove that the level of threat was higher than usual. The temporary intensification of security screening procedures, such as the procedures instituted in response to threats to air travel security at New York airports, appear to have been received by air carriers and the traveling public with little clamor.

Because of the strong relationship between public acceptance and the perception of risk, the panel believes the FAA should make this link explicit in a strategy for implementing new passenger screening technologies. Because it is impossible to predict the course that terrorism will take in the coming years, the FAA plan should include relating specific technologies to specific threats. As threat scenarios shift with changing national and international climates, this information would make it possible for the FAA to implement technologies quickly in response to specific threats. The FAA plan should also include information on how new technologies will be implemented over time in the absence of specific threats against U.S. air carriers or airports.

By immediately addressing the link between the perceived level of threat and the acceptance of more intrusive security screening processes, the FAA will help air carriers react more quickly to specific threats. Air carriers will also be able to plan for the purchase of equipment based on new technologies as part of their routine efforts to upgrade security screening equipment.

ASSESSMENT OF PUBLIC ACCEPTANCE

The panel can formulate some general conclusions and recommendations about new technologies for passenger screening. However, further steps must be taken to assess public acceptance and to incorporate information from these assessments into screening procedures for each technology under investigation to ensure that it is suitable for use in passenger screening. Assessing public attitudes is also important because, as the panel workshop clearly revealed, limited data are available on public opinion even regarding the implementation of current screening technologies. Because the successful implementation of a new screening technology will be influenced by the public attitude, data on public opinion must be obtained for all proposed screening technologies. Identifying possible blocks to implementation early in the development process will cost less than retrofitting a fully developed system to address particular concerns.

Assessing the potential for public acceptance of a new screening system or procedure is a complex problem for two main reasons. First, it is more difficult to determine public reaction to an abstract, proposed system than to a real, here-and-now piece of equipment. Therefore, it will be important for the FAA to assess public reaction to new screening systems and procedures while the systems are still being developed and when prototypes are available for demonstration. Second, the previously discussed link between the level of threat and the acceptability of more intrusive screening procedures must be taken into account. The results of surveys or other measures of potential public acceptance will be affected by the prevailing level of threat. A carefully designed survey may be able to account for the influence of perceived threat.

Insight can be gained from studies of public reactions to, and acceptance of, current metal detectors and baggage screening systems when they were first introduced. More recently, imaging systems were introduced in correctional institutions to screen individuals entering the facility by producing images of their bodies beneath their clothes. Experience with these systems can provide insight on public reactions to, and acceptance of, this type of passenger-system interface.

Finally, armed with information about public reactions to specific screening technologies, a public education campaign to address specific concerns can be formulated to improve acceptance of a new technology. Information about specific technologies must be presented in a way that is understandable to a variety of audiences. Analogies to other common or familiar experiences are often effective.

TECHNOLOGICAL IMPROVEMENTS

A major problem with current passenger screening technologies and procedures is that they do not provide the operator with specific information about the nature and location of potential threat items. New technologies designed to assist operators to locate and identify objects identified by the equipment as potential threats should address the following concerns:

- *Convenience.* Passengers will experience less delay if operators can quickly determine whether or not the item that triggered the alarm is a threat.
- *Privacy.* Operators will be less likely to encounter external medical devices or other nonthreat objects that passengers consider personal, if the equipment is designed to identify the location of the item that triggered the alarm.

- *Legal.* Information about nonthreat items will be minimized by limiting the search area. This will also lessen the need for a policy on discovery of illegal, but nonthreat, items.[1]

Improvements to Current Technologies

Improvements to current metal-detection technologies are not likely to be apparent to the traveling public or to operators of the screening equipment. However, screening systems that will improve the ability of the operator to identify threat objects quickly and accurately could address concerns identified above. The panel did not identify other concerns related to improvements in metal-detection technology.

Technologies to Address Future Passenger Screening Requirements

The trade-off between technology performance and public acceptance is an issue for all technological improvements in airport security screening. Any changes to the now-familiar metal-detection portals will cause concerns over health effects, the invasion of privacy, and passenger convenience.

Imaging Technologies

Imaging technologies can *see through* clothes and produce an image of the human body underneath. The images vary in the amount of detail they present, depending on the technology, but none is of *photographic quality*. Operators then view and interpret these images. Concerns about improving operator effectiveness for current screening systems, discussed below, may apply to using imaging technologies as well.

Imaging technologies can be classified as either *passive* or *active*. In passive screening, the natural radiation emitted by the human body is detected and analyzed. This procedure minimizes concerns about radiation. Active imaging entails irradiating the body with x-rays or millimeter waves and analyzing the radiation scattered from the body. In both imaging procedures, objects (e.g., metallic weapons or explosive materials) that emit or scatter radiation differently from the human body will appear different from the background on the image. At the current level of development of imaging technologies, images must be viewed and interpreted by an operator. Many of the concerns discussed below would be

---

[1] Current legal interpretation holds that the screening of passengers and others as they enter an airport or concourse is allowable only when the search is performed to identify items that are a threat to aviation security. Air carriers are not authorized to search for other illegal or suspicious items, such as drugs or large amounts of cash, that do not endanger the aircraft.

mitigated by the development of effective, automated image-interpretation capabilities that would eliminate the operator from the routine screening process.

The panel concluded that the images produced by these technologies are of sufficiently high quality to make them effective for screening passengers. However, when the perceived level of threat is low, passengers, crews, and others passing through screening checkpoints are likely to object to having images of their bodies displayed. There are also likely to be concerns about the use and storage of the data used to generate images. Procedures, such as having operators of the same sex view the images or moving operators away from the screening checkpoints, could allay concerns. However, for financial and logistical reasons, these procedures are likely to make imaging technologies extremely unattractive for use as primary screening systems at all checkpoints. Quantifying the level of threat at which people are likely to accept this kind of invasion of privacy is difficult but necessary prior to mandating the use of any imaging technology for screening passengers at airports.

Because active imaging technologies use the detection of various forms of radiation to create the images, there are also likely to be concerns about health effects. The panel concluded that the levels of radiation exposure required for image production are insignificant compared to the levels experienced during many other common activities, including airplane flights. Therefore, health concerns associated with imaging technologies have more to do with the perception among certain segments of the population, such as frequent travelers or pregnant women, that these radiation levels are harmful. These perceptions can be addressed by a public education campaign and by offering equally effective alternative screening procedures for those who do not want to be irradiated.

Trace-Detection Technologies

Trace-detection technologies physically collect samples of air or material from clothing or bodies of individuals and use the samples to infer the presence of dangerous materials. Sample collection can entail sampling the air around individuals or touching them to remove particles of explosive materials from them or their belongings. Chemical compounds of interest can be identified using many techniques. The specifics of the chemical-identification technologies are less likely to cause passenger concern than the sample collection techniques.

Unlike imaging technologies, where the technologies themselves are mature and the equipment is commercially available, trace-detection technologies are still in the development phase, especially with regard to methods of sample collection and matching appropriate sampling techniques with chemical-identification technologies. Therefore, it is more difficult for the panel to comment on specific passenger screening scenarios involving trace-detection technologies.

However, sample collection for trace-detection technologies must entail the physical transfer of material from the person being screened to the screening equipment. Sampling the air around a person is less intrusive, but likely to be less effective, than touching the person to collect a sample. For technologies that require touching, one concern is people's aversion to being touched either by inanimate objects, such as bars or fronds, or by operators wielding hand-wand devices. This concern is difficult to address because the desire to preserve distance from strangers is deeply ingrained and is often influenced by basic cultural and religious beliefs. The *optimum* distance people maintain between themselves and others varies greatly from person to person and from culture to culture, and it is not likely to be changed by public information campaigns. Concerns about privacy, about initiating physical contact, and the transmission of disease may prove to be significant hurdles to implementing new technologies.

Trace-detection technologies are also being considered for use in screening hand-carried baggage and personal electronic devices. Objections to touching these items are likely to be less intense than objections to touching people themselves. Collecting samples from areas that a person is likely to have touched may be an effective way of transporting material from that person to the screening equipment. Collecting samples from boarding cards may be a practical way of implementing trace-detection technologies in passenger screening.

ROLE OF OPERATORS IN PASSENGER SCREENING

The panel determined that the involvement of security personnel and the quality of their performance are critical elements in the successful implementation of a security system. Operators are responsible for the decision-making component of the security system. The sound analytical capability of operators is a major requirement for accurately determining the potential danger to the aircraft.

The FAA Human Factors Program has begun to formulate objective criteria for selecting, training, and motivating screening personnel. It is frequently assumed that poor performance of current security systems can be attributed to the low wages paid to operators. It is further assumed that higher wages would attract *better* personnel and result in significant improvements in performance. However, the panel members believe that other more powerful reasons are to blame for the less-than-desirable operator performance reported by the FAA (Fobes, 1995). At best, higher wages may mean less turnover among operators (a severe problem in itself), providing opportunities to apply better selection, training, and motivational methods.

Competent operator performance in new passenger screening systems will depend on the combined effect of programs dealing with operator ergonomics, selection, training, and motivation. Techniques for measuring operator performance are critical to the success of a program for assessing prototype systems, validating operator selection methods, evaluating new training techniques, monitoring and analyzing the on-line effectiveness of security-screening systems and personnel, and providing feedback to individual operators.

The allocation of functions between machine and operator is likely to have a significant influence on the effectiveness of future systems. In an apparent paradox, as screening systems become more automated, operator performance is likely to become even more important to the successful implementation of these systems. Operators will be performing more difficult and complex tasks that defy automation, and increased automation will introduce a host of new human performance issues. In developing new screening technologies, it would be more practical to integrate the proper allocation of functions into the technology development cycle itself, rather than to address the integration of the human operator into the system after the equipment has been designed and tested.

To aid air carriers and screening companies in selecting, training, and motivating passenger screening personnel and to provide direction on the use of ergonomics in designing security-screening equipment, the panel recommends that the FAA accelerate its program in human factors. The program can assist in developing effective measurements of operator performance, determining the optimal allocation of functions in new systems during development, and integrating research on operator ergonomics, selection, training, and motivation into the explosives-detection program. Successful implementation of any passenger screening system, based on current technologies or on a proposed new technology, requires the effective integration of human operators into the overall security system.

1

Introduction

DEVELOPMENT OF AVIATION SECURITY

Two major events caused the public to exert pressure on the U.S. government to implement security procedures at airports and to mandate security requirements for U.S. air carriers. The first was the increase in the incidence of hijackings during the late 1960s and early 1970s (see figure 1-1), which resulted in the establishment of Anti-Hijacking Program of the Federal Aviation Administration (FAA). The second event was the destruction of Pan American Airlines Flight 103 over Lockerbie, Scotland, on December 21, 1988, which resulted in the creation of the President's Commission on Airline Security and Terrorism in 1989 and the enactment of the recommendations of that commission into the Aviation Security Improvement Act of 1990 (Public Law 101-604).

FAA Anti-Hijacking Program

On September 11, 1970, President Richard Nixon announced "a program to deal with airplane hijacking," which ordered air carriers to deploy "surveillance equipment and techniques to all appropriate airports in the United States." The president further instructed the Departments of Defense and Transportation to work with the U.S. air carrier industry to determine if metal detectors and x-ray devices used by the military could assist in preventing hijackings. On February 1, 1972, the FAA issued a rule requiring air carriers to use a screening system, acceptable to the FAA, that would require screening all passengers "by one or more of the following systems: behavioral profile, magnetometer, identification check, physical search." Hijackings continued and on December 5, 1972, the FAA issued emergency rules that required screening all passengers and carry-on baggage on all certified, scheduled passenger aircraft. The anti-hijacking or screening program currently used by U.S. air carriers is almost identical to the program initiated in 1972. This program requires air carriers to implement a security program capable of preventing the introduction of weapons and explosive or incendiary devices aboard an aircraft. Since the issuance of this rule, the screening program has been improved in terms of training procedures, x-ray and metal-detector standards, access control specifications, employment standards, and testing requirements.

As a result of the increased incidence of hijacking and sabotage of U.S. air carriers in the past quarter century, numerous statutes, treaties, and regulations have been promulgated by a variety of entities to establish the current U.S. civil aviation security system (see appendix A). Air carriers, airports, and the FAA each have specific roles to play in ensuring airport security, as outlined in table 1-1.

PASSENGER SCREENING

Approximately 1.5 million commercial aviation passengers are screened in the United States each day for weapons and dangerous articles prior to boarding an airplane. Passengers place their carry-on baggage on a conveyor belt for inspection by x-ray equipment, and they walk through a portal that detects the presence of metallic objects. If the metal-detecting portal sounds an alarm, passengers are searched further to determine the cause of the alarm and to ensure that they are not carrying objects that could be a threat to aviation security. These alarm-clearing search procedures employ either a hand-wand metal detector or a physical pat-down search. The technologies for detecting metallic objects are mature, and the manner in which these technologies are implemented to ensure airport and air carrier security is familiar to travelers.

However, these technologies are not capable of detecting nonmetallic weapons, plastic explosives, and other dangerous materials. The FAA is working to make current technologies more effective and to develop new technologies with wider applicability. As these new technologies mature, issues regarding their implementation in airports, including passenger acceptance and air carrier and airport accommodation, will become important factors in determining which technologies will be appropriate for airport use.

The Panel on Passenger Screening investigated a variety of nontechnology issues related to the implementation of new screening technologies to assist the FAA in identifying the most promising technologies. The panel reviewed potential screening devices or methods currently under consideration by the FAA for use in airports. The panel also assessed aspects of each method that could cause public concern over such issues as health risks involved (e.g., exposure to radiation), privacy, and traveler comfort, in light of current and

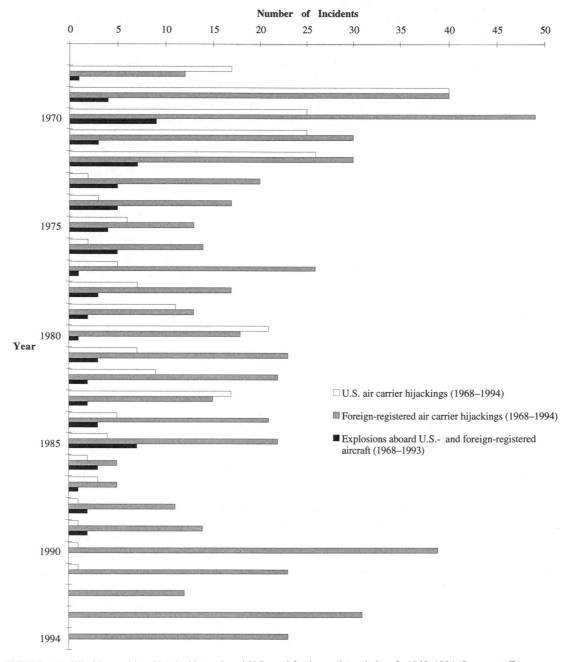

FIGURE 1-1   Hijacking and bombing incidents aboard U.S.- and foreign-registered aircraft, 1968–1994. Sources: ATA (n.d.); FAA (1993).

anticipated health regulations, and privacy laws. The panel considered ways in which the methods could be implemented to maintain high levels of effectiveness, while minimizing health risks and increasing public acceptance. The panel also identified key factors that could affect their implementation, considering mitigating strategies and alternate screening methods for those passengers who wish to avoid

the automated system. Methods for clearing alarms also were discussed.

Because both current and new technologies require security personnel to supplement the automated system when a passenger sets off the alarm, the panel considered the operator as an integral part of the entire passenger screening system.

TABLE 1-1   Responsibilities of Air Carriers, Airport Operators, and the FAA for Passenger Screening

Entity	Responsibility	Action
Air carriers	Provide secure travel	Maintain security program Screen passengers/carry-on baggage Secure baggage/cargo Protect/secure aircraft
Airports	Provide secure operating environment	Maintain security program Protect operations area Provide law enforcement support
FAA	Provide administrative and procedural guidance	Identify/analyze threats Establish requirements/procedures Coordinate crisis situations Provide technical assistance Enforce regulations
Passengers	Cooperate	Fund carrier/airport security via travel purchase

Sources: ATA (n.d.); ATA (1984); FAA (1975); FAA (1981); 14 C.F.R. §107.20 (1995); *United States v. Davis* (1973).

Operation of Passenger Screening Systems

The FAA integrates information from the intelligence community, policymakers, air carriers, and airports to determine the level of threat to civil aviation. When no specific threat has been identified, the security system operates at a basic level for detecting weapons and explosives on passengers or in their baggage. Low alert levels[1] indicate that the FAA considers the probability of an attempted bombing or hijacking to be minimal. If specific hijacking or terrorist targets have been identified, the FAA declares a higher alert level and warns air carriers and airport authorities of the specific bomb or hijacking threats and of their potential locations. For higher alert levels, the security-screening process imposes additional procedures to increase the likelihood of detecting the terrorist. Rapidly changing situations may require significant modifications in screening procedures, with little or no advanced warning. These procedures involve more thorough screening, including additional baggage inspection, passenger questioning, and identification checks.

The level of tolerance demonstrated by the traveling public for the inconvenience, lack of privacy, perceived health risks, and delays for passengers, greeters, and air crews will be proportional to their perception of the severity of the threat. More expensive screening equipment and more intrusive screening procedures will be acceptable at higher alert levels, but only if the threat is perceived to warrant them and if the equipment or procedures are perceived to be effective in deterring the threat. The dilemma in passenger screening is how to provide an effective and suitable level of screening at a reasonable cost for all threat levels.

The performance of a security system must be evaluated to determine both its effectiveness and suitability. Effectiveness is the capability to detect threat objects, and it is generally dependent on the capabilities of the system technology. Suitability is the capability of the system to operate with few undesirable characteristics (e.g., elevated radiation levels). Performance should be evaluated continually, and the process should be designed to provide feedback to allow air carriers and equipment manufacturers to improve the effectiveness and suitability of a system.

Compliance with standards set by the FAA is considered the minimum acceptable level of performance. For example, when metal-detection portals are first installed in an airport or moved to a new location, they must be proven to perform at the minimum compliance level specified by the FAA. Screening systems are evaluated for both equipment and system compliance to ensure a minimum level of performance. Evaluation includes testing the ability of the system to detect, react to, and properly respond to a terrorist threat or action. For example, system compliance may be determined by using government *red teams* to test airport systems, as

---

[1]The FAA has defined specific aviation security (AVSEC) alert levels and the circumstances justifying the declaration of higher alert levels. These definitions are considered sensitive information. The descriptions used here are generally illustrative of the FAA alert levels.

HIJACKINGS

The first recorded hijacking of a U.S. air carrier occurred in 1961. Hijacking was a rare event until 1968, when 17 hijackings, mostly to Cuba, were attempted in the United States.

BOMBINGS

The first recorded sabotage of a commercial aircraft occurred on May 7, 1949. A Philippine Airlines plane flying from Daet to Manila, Philippines, crashed into the sea after a bomb exploded on board. The incident resulted from a domestic dispute in which a woman hired assassins to kill her husband, who was on the aircraft. The first bombing incident involving a U.S. commercial carrier occurred on November 1, 1955, when a United Airlines plane crashed shortly after takeoff from Denver, Colorado, after a bomb exploded in the luggage of a passenger. The passenger's son had planned the event in order to collect on an insurance policy. During a 40-year period, from 1949 to 1989, in-flight explosions have resulted in the deaths of 2,102 people.

---

described to the panel by a former head of security for El Al Airlines (Issacharoff, 1995). The Panel on Passenger Screening concentrated on the suitability of new technologies and paid particular attention to the interrelationship between suitability and effectiveness.

KEY ISSUES

Current passenger security-screening requirements were established as a result of the pre-1972 increase in the number of hijackings. These requirements focus on the ability to find passengers carrying metallic weapons that may be used to intimidate the air crew into changing the destination of an aircraft. However, with increasing international political unrest and the attractiveness of U.S. aircraft as terrorist targets, the FAA has recognized the need to expand airport security-screening processes to include the detection of plastic explosives and other threat objects or substances. This need is the driving force behind the development of new screening technologies.

A number of issues are associated with the suitability and effectiveness of new airport passenger screening technologies. A main issue, which relates to suitability, is *reliability*, i.e., the consistency of the performance of the system. A second issue, related to effectiveness, is *fidelity*, i.e., how accurately the output from the system represents the item being examined. A system with high fidelity

provides sufficiently detailed and accurate information to enable the operator to make correct judgments and appropriate decisions regarding the presence of objects the system is designed to detect. Low reliability or fidelity levels result in poor system performance, including false alarms and the failure to detect harmful objects.

In addition to the technological aspects of passenger screening systems, there are also reliability issues associated with the operating personnel. Sound operator judgment and decision-making capabilities are critical to successful passenger screening. Operator inaccuracies and inconsistencies can also result in the failure of a system to detect harmful objects and in false alarms, which translate into unacceptable system performance. Personnel requirements are typically addressed through selection[2] and training.

Whether or not a new screening technology will be acceptable to the public is a question that involves a number of significant issues. It should be noted that the term *public* does not refer to a homogeneous group. Although in this report the panel refers to the typical person being screened as a *passenger*, the population exposed to screening is actually broader. It includes air passengers, friends and relatives of passengers, flight crews, and airport employees. Some people are exposed to screening quite infrequently, while others, who often travel by air, are screened more frequently. People exposed to screening technologies can be expected to express concerns in four areas:

- health—typified by perceived health risks associated with exposure to x-rays
- convenience—usually a matter of delays; as delays become longer, public acceptance of a particular screening procedure decreases
- privacy—for both an individual's body and possessions; technologies that display images of the body or that involve person-to-person contact raise potential concerns about privacy
- comfort—the physical intrusion of the screening equipment on the passenger

Because people differ in terms of the importance they place on the various concerns discussed above, they will also differ in their level of acceptance or rejection of passenger screening technologies. Issues of health, convenience, and privacy are important, but the *distribution* of public response to these issues is equally important. Aside from considering the types of reactions new screening technologies may elicit, the FAA will have to define *acceptable* levels of opposition. That is, a certain proportion of the public will oppose the implementation of any new technology, and the FAA will

---

[2]Selection involves identifying people capable of functioning, or of being trained to function, as operators at an acceptable level.

have to weigh the need for more effective airport security against the known opposition before mandating implementation of a new technology.

Widespread acceptance of a new screening technology is not simply a matter of how people respond or what percentage of the population accepts or rejects the procedure. Rather, acceptance can be viewed properly as a trade-off by the public; that is, each person will perform a personal costs-benefits analysis between the perceived threat and the benefits of a higher level of security screening. Thus, the extent to which a screening procedure is viewed as successful in providing security and the degree to which security is seen as a necessity are important factors in public acceptance.

A final point to be noted concerns the matter of choice. Where more than one screening technology is available at a particular screening point, people who object to a primary procedure, such as a technique that displays an image of the human body under clothing, may be given the option of a secondary procedure, such as searching with a hand-wand device. Although making such options available may be costly in terms of money and efficiency, doing so will alleviate many concerns. Screening technologies provide security by detecting objects, but they also function as deterrents. Their effectiveness as deterrents depends on perceived, rather than actual, reliability and fidelity.

In gathering data for this report, the panel assumed that each screening technology, at a basic level, performed the job it was designed to do. That is, the panel did not address the technical issues related to improving hardware technologies. Instead, the panel focused on the broader issues of passenger and airport or air carrier concerns that could arise with the implementation of new technologies. In the report, the panel notes instances where addressing a specific concern would decrease the effectiveness of a technology.

The panel also assumed that the technology under consideration will be used as the primary passenger screening technology or one through which all passengers will be examined. However, if the FAA and the air carriers can develop a reliable method for determining which passengers pose no danger to the flight, for example, by developing an effective passenger-profiling system, then new technologies may be used as a secondary screening system for more intensive inspection of passengers who cannot be cleared in advance. Thus, development of a passenger-profiling system holds great promise.

This report addresses three general categories of passenger screening technologies: imaging technologies, trace-detection technologies, and nonimaging electromagnetic technologies. Chapter 2 summarizes the methodology the panel used to evaluate the concerns associated with new technologies. Chapter 3 addresses the individual technology types in greater depth. Chapter 4 outlines the operating conditions under which new passenger screening technologies will have to operate. Chapter 5 discusses the role of human operators in security systems and how that role could change to improve total system performance. The final chapters, 6, 7, and 8, discuss the primary concerns (i.e., health effects, privacy concerns, and public acceptance) associated with new technologies. The panel's conclusions and recommendations are presented in chapter 9.

2

Methodology

The Panel on Passenger Screening developed this report based on: (1) committee meetings and technical literature provided to the committee by the FAA and the National Research Council (NRC) staff, (2) presentations by outside experts who briefed the panel on specific passenger screening technologies and implementation and operational issues, and (3) a workshop on passenger screening during which several outside organizations presented their views and concerns. Panel members were also invited to meetings of the NRC Committee on Aviation Security, which oversaw this study, to hear presentations by experts on various aspects of passenger screening technologies, explosives detection systems, and security issues concerning both passengers and baggage. The panel membership included experts in human factors, risk perception and psychology, imaging science, electrical engineering, chemical detection, health effects of radiation, and legal issues.

PANEL MEETINGS

The panel conducted five meetings between February and September 1995 to gather information used in developing this report. In preparation for these meetings, the panelists received technical and nontechnical literature on various aspects of passenger screening technologies for their review and consideration. Information was provided by the FAA and by outside experts, who are listed in table 2-1.

WORKSHOP ON PASSENGER SCREENING

The panel held the Workshop on New Technologies for Passenger Screening to gain a broader perspective on health, privacy, comfort, and other concerns regarding passenger screening from organizations interested in air travel safety. The workshop was held on June 3, 1995, at the NRC Georgetown facilities in Washington, D.C. Panel members, FAA staff, and representatives of other organizations participated in the workshop (see table 2-2). These representatives also provided the panel with written comments contained in appendix B.

At the workshop, the panel members discussed passenger screening issues (particularly issues related to health and privacy) with representatives of professional associations and interest groups. The panel considered the contributions of workshop participants excellent and useful. However, screening technologies were discussed only in general, and the

TABLE 2-1   Speakers and Topics Presented to the Panel on Passenger Screening

Speaker	Affiliation	Topic
Douglas Smith	U.S. Customs Service	Technology for contraband detection
Art Janata	Pacific Northwest Laboratories	Chemical sensor options
Nicholas Virca	Nicolet Imaging Systems	Technology of the Secure 1000
Dale Murray	Sandia National Laboratories	Electromagnetic portal technology
Dan Issacharoff	Consultant	Risk analysis system used by El Al
Ray Smietan	U.S. Department of Justice	Department of Defense/Department of Justice weapons detection program
James Fobes	FAA	FAA human factors program
Paul Jankowski	FAA	FAA research and development
Frank Fox	FAA	FAA in-house research and development

TABLE 2-2 Organizations at the Workshop on New Technologies for Passenger Screening

Organization	Representative
Air Transport Association of America (Washington, D.C.)	S. Rork
Airport Law Enforcement Agents Network (Dallas-Fort Worth Airport, Texas)	A. Dodson
American Association of Airport Executives (Alexandria, Va.)	A. Graser
Airports Council International North America (Washington, D.C.)	A. Graser
American Civil Liberties Union (Washington, D.C.)	D. Haines
Association of Flight Attendants (Washington, D.C.)	M. Leith
Aviation Consumer Action Project (Washington, D.C.)	G. Frankosky
ITS, a provider of airport security personnel and services (Cleveland, Ohio)	S. Dennison
Regional Airline Association (Washington, D.C.)	D. McElroy

Organizations invited but not attending:
Air Line Pilots Association, International
Allied Pilots Association
American Society of Travel Agents
Electronic Privacy Information Center
Families of Pan Am 103 Lockerbie
Victims of Pan Am 103

opinions of the participants should be used as a starting point for investigating concerns about specific technologies. In addition, these opinions may not be typical of opinions held by all professional associations, interest groups, or the public. A summary and analysis of the workshop are presented in chapter 8 of this report.

It was evident from discussions at the workshop that data is needed on public opinion regarding the implementation of passenger-screening technologies. Little is known even about public attitudes toward the implementation of current systems. Public opinion will certainly influence the successful deployment of new screening technologies. Therefore, it is important to determine potential public attitudes toward proposed screening technologies before implementation.

SUMMARY

To address the issues outlined in the report, the Panel on Passenger Screening relied on the expertise of panel members and on input from various other sources. These sources included airport and air carrier personnel and organizations and individuals concerned with both the safe operation of aircraft and the interests of the traveling public.

3

Passenger Screening Technologies

Perceptions of increased threats from explosives and non-metallic weapons have prompted the investigation of new passenger screening technologies, including chemical trace-detection techniques and imaging methods that can *see through* clothing. The development of these technologies has reached the stage at which operational implementation can be contemplated. However, possible negative public reaction toward many of these new detection technologies will have to be addressed before these systems can be used in airports. Demands for additional space, utilities, labor costs, and increased operator skills that these technologies could impose on air carriers and airports also will have to be considered. This chapter describes the technological aspects of the systems under consideration.

Screening procedures currently used in U.S. airports, at least during routine operations, involve metal-detection portals for screening passengers and x-ray imaging systems for screening hand-carried baggage. Metal-detection devices impose a time-varying magnetic field in the space within the portal that induces eddy currents in metallic or ferromagnetic objects passing through that space. Various methods are used to detect these eddy currents, and when they exceed a preset level, an operator intervenes to ascertain the presence or absence of a dangerous object or weapon. The effectiveness of this security screening system depends not only on the performance of the equipment, but also on the performance of the personnel operating the equipment and resolving the alarms.

The detection instrumentation can be adjusted to optimize its ability to detect specific metals or alloys. The FAA utilizes a number of specific weapons to test the proper operation and performance of these metal-detection units. Typically, instruments are tuned for the optimum detection of these FAA test objects, at the expense of reducing instrument sensitivity in detecting weapons or objects not contained in this set of specific test weapons.

The FAA is considering for future application several new technologies capable of detecting a wider range of threat objects. The following section describes an approach used by a foreign air carrier, followed by sections describing the new technologies being considered by the FAA.

PASSENGER-PROFILING SYSTEM

Among the presentations to the panel was a particularly enlightening one by Dan Issacharoff, the former head of

security for El Al Airlines of Israel. Because of its national affiliation, El Al has frequently been a terrorist target. In response, El Al has developed an extensive security program requiring inspection of all baggage and the face-to-face questioning of all passengers. Issacharoff said the El Al security system emphasizes the identification of people who could be a threat, rather than the detection of objects that could be used to hijack or destroy an airplane. The system used to identify people who could be a threat is illustrated in figure 3-1, which identifies five types of people who could pose a threat to an airplane, ranging from *naive terrorists*, passengers who are unaware that they are carrying dangerous objects, to *suicide terrorists* who intentionally carry dangerous objects to destroy the airplane and kill everyone on board, including themselves. El Al has also developed psychological profiles of these individuals and a passenger-interrogation technique designed to identify them during check-in and before boarding.

This system has worked well for El Al, but Issacharoff pointed out that El Al flies out of approximately 200 airports worldwide. In contrast, U.S. air carriers operate more flights out of more than 400 airports in the United States alone. In addition, a large number of El Al passengers travel on international flights and arrive at the airport early enough to allow time for security screening. The time- and personnel-intensive system used by El Al may be suitable for international flights, but it would be inappropriate for an operation the size

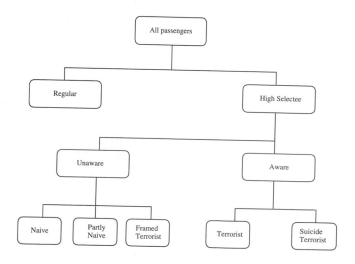

FIGURE 3-1 El Al Airlines system for identifying people who could be threats.

13

TABLE 3-1   Passenger Screening Technologies Based on Imaging

Detection technology	Uses	Comments
Millimeter waves	Portals	Requires more than a single view
	Wall units	Requires more than a single view
	Enclosed spaces	Could get a 360° view
X-rays	Portals	Requires more than a single view
	Enclosed spaces	Could get a 360° view

Source: Jankowski (1995a, b).

of the U.S. domestic air travel industry. However, the El Al screening system could serve as a model for a passenger-profiling method to help air carriers identify passengers who require more extensive screening.

IMAGING TECHNOLOGIES

Several emerging technologies can detect metallic and nonmetallic weapons, explosives, and other contraband material concealed under multiple layers of clothing by creating images that can be examined to discern these materials. No physical contact is involved. These are already used for a wide variety of security applications, such as screening visitors to correctional facilities and exit-screening employees to deter theft. Table 3-1 outlines some of the ways imaging devices could be implemented in an airport environment.

Imaging technologies either scan subjects for natural radiation emitted by the human body (passive imaging) or expose subjects to a specific type of radiation reflected by the body (active imaging). In either case, materials such as metallic weapons or plastic explosives, which emit or reflect radiation differently from the human body, are distinguishable from the background image of the body. These screening systems generate television-like digital images that can be

evaluated by image processing and analysis methods. Images are viewed by an operator trained to identify potential threat objects in these images, sometimes with the assistance of image enhancing software that highlights unusual features. Although these technologies cannot detect objects concealed inside the body or in skin flaps, they are being considered for airport passenger screening because they would enable air carriers to screen for a wider variety of materials than they can with present screening systems. Two technologies under consideration use either x-ray or millimeter (or submillimeter) wavelength electromagnetic radiation. Figure 3-2 shows the electromagnetic spectrum, indicating the wavelength of x-ray and millimeter wave radiation in relation to other common sources of electromagnetic radiation.[1]

Passive Millimeter-Wave Imaging

A passive technology under investigation by the FAA operates in the millimeter-wave range (near 100 gigahertz) of

---

[1]Energy, frequency, and wavelength are fundamentally related. Energy is inversely proportional to wavelength (e.g., long wavelength radiation is low energy and low frequency; short wavelength radiation is high energy and high frequency).

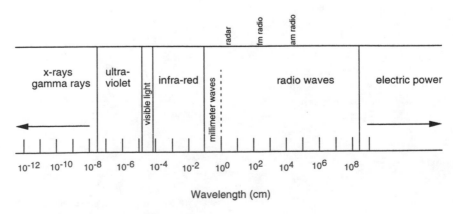

FIGURE 3-2 The electromagnetic spectrum.

 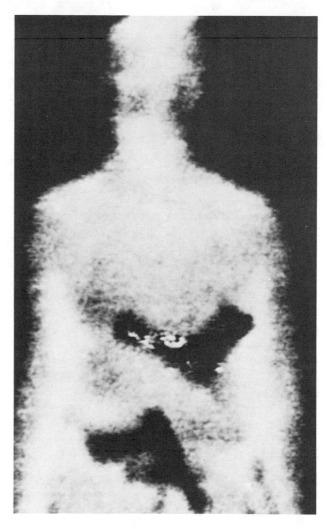

FIGURE 3-3a   Visual image of a person being scanned by the Contraband Detection System produced by Millitech.
FIGURE 3-3b   Millimeter-wave image of the same person showing two weapons hidden under the subject's sweater.
Reproduced courtesy of Millitech Corporation (1995).

the electromagnetic spectrum. Passive millimeter-wave imaging is based on the principle that any object not at absolute zero temperature emits electromagnetic energy at all wavelengths. This energy can be detected by an appropriate receiver and can be used to produce an image. An important feature of this technology is its ability to accomplish imaging by gathering the radiation emitted naturally from the human body without artificial radiation. Thus, no health risks are associated with this technology. (An in-depth discussion of health concerns is presented in chapter 6.) The display methods and privacy considerations of passive millimeter-wave imaging techniques are similar to those of the x-ray methods described later in this chapter.

Figure 3-3a shows the visual image of a person being scanned using the Contraband Detection System produced by Millitech. Figure 3-3b is the resulting screening image showing the outline of two guns hidden under the subject's sweater. Images of this type reveal items a passenger might normally carry, such as a wallet, keys, a pocket knife, and belt buckles. Effective image analysis and interpretation requires these and other common and nonthreatening items to be distinguishable from threat objects. Images of subjects carrying threat objects, such as the ones shown in this report, were taken to illustrate the capabilities of the technology. They are not representative of typical airline passengers carrying a variety of objects that clutter their screen images. Image-analysis software is being developed to facilitate interpretation, but current technology requires interpretation by human operators.

Active Millimeter-Wave Imaging

Active millimeter-wave imaging technologies operate as short-range radar systems that project a narrow beam of millimeter-wavelength energy against the target and detect the reflected rays. The beam is scanned from head-to-toe or toe-to-head to produce an image of the subject. Battelle Pacific Northwest Laboratories is developing a system for screening people based on active millimeter-wave technology. This method involves illuminating the subject with millimeter-wave radiation, but at a level low enough to prevent adverse health effects. However, the popular perception of the dangers of microwave radiation may cause public concern over this imaging technique.

Active X-ray Imaging

Active x-ray imaging technology uses low-energy, low-intensity x-rays reflected from the subject to create an image. The images are interpreted to detect the presence of metallic and nonmetallic weapons and explosives concealed under multiple layers of clothing. Two companies, Nicolet Imaging Systems in California and American Science and Engineering, Inc. (AS&E), in Massachusetts, now produce systems used for personnel screening.

Figure 3-4 is a representative photograph of an x-ray screening system. Figures 3-5 and 3-6 are examples of images from active x-ray imaging systems.[2] The images are revealing, but, as mentioned earlier, the subject is probably not representative of passengers who usually carry more nonthreat items on their persons. As in passive imaging systems, the presence of these nonthreat items makes images produced by x-ray imaging systems difficult to analyze and interpret.

Assessment of Imaging Technologies

The effectiveness of these technologies depends on how distinct the threat objects can be made against the background and how much of the body can be screened. Although the technologies being considered cannot create a *photographic quality* image, they can produce images that trained operators can interpret. All current imaging technologies require operators to view the images because humans can interpret complex images and identify anomalous objects more efficiently than available software. The wide variety of human shapes and sizes that can be expected during everyday screening also complicates automated image interpretation because software cannot simply be taught to recognize and discount a *standard human body*.

Another factor affecting the effectiveness of imaging technologies is the amount of time required to obtain enough information to make a decision. In screening passengers, the

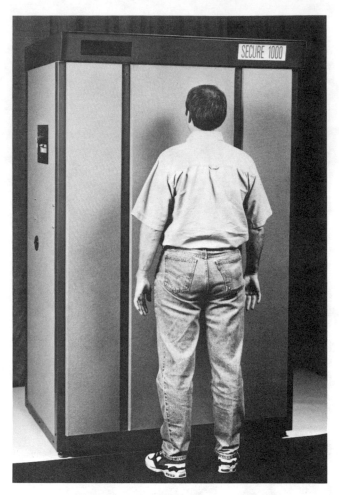

FIGURE 3-4   Person being scanned (front image) using the SECURE 1000 active x-ray imaging system produced by Nicolet Imaging Systems. Reproduced courtesy of Nicolet Imaging Systems (1995).

target processing time is six seconds, which is the approximate time required to examine a passenger's hand-carried baggage. Each image shown in figure 3-5 was produced in three seconds; this plus the time required for image interpretation determines total processing time. In current applications of imaging technologies, including systems at correctional facilities, images from at least two sides—front and back—are usually taken. Images may also be taken from both sides, often with the subject's arms raised, to provide a 360° view. It is likely that there is less time pressure when screening people entering a correctional facility than when screening people preparing to board an airplane.

TRACE-DETECTION TECHNOLOGIES

Trace-detection technologies are based on the direct chemical identification of either particles of explosive material or vapor containing explosive material. Thus, the presence of a threat object or bomb is inferred from the presence

---

[2]These images are created using x-rays reflected off the surface of the body. X-ray images used by doctors for diagnoses are created using much higher energy x-rays transmitted through the body.

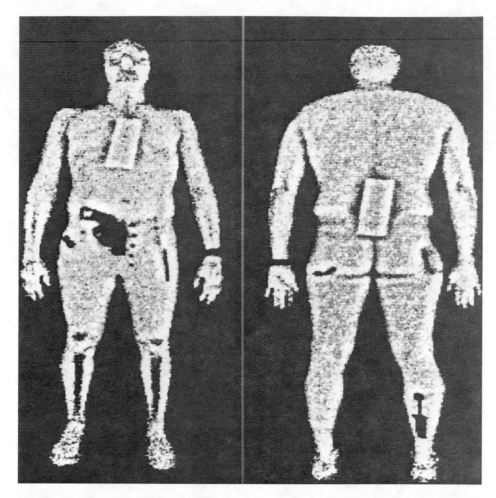

FIGURE 3-5   Image created by the SECURE 1000, produced by Nicolet Imaging Systems, showing several threat objects, including a half-pound simulated explosive charge and a .38 caliber handgun. Reproduced courtesy of Nicolet Imaging Systems (1995).

of particulate matter or vapor. The main difference between trace-detection and electromagnetic or imaging is that in trace detection, a sample of the explosive material must be transported to the instrument in concentrations that exceed the detection limit. Trace-detection technologies cannot be used to detect the presence of metallic weapons.

The two distinct steps in trace detection are sample collection and chemical identification. To identify the presence of explosives, both steps have to function at the same time. The sample-collection phase of the procedure is the main point of contact between the technology and the subjects being screened. Table 3-2 shows potential applications of trace-detection equipment in airports.

Sample Collection

Explosive substances can be transported from the carrier to the detection instrument as vapor or as solid particles.

Initial efforts in the development of trace-detection technology were focused on collecting vapor around the person or baggage. However, because many modern explosives do not readily give off vapor at room temperature, the focus has expanded to include detection of particulates of explosive materials on the skin and other surfaces.

If traces of explosive material are to be detected, they must be concentrated from an air sample (vapor technologies) or dislodged from a substrate (particulate technologies). In vapor detection, large amounts of air must be collected, from which small amounts of the substances of interest must be extracted. In particle detection, pieces of explosive material must be removed from the surface to which they are adhering. Both trace-detection approaches have strengths and weaknesses, depending on the type of explosive material being sought. Vapor technologies are more effective for detecting explosive materials with high vapor pressures, while particulate technologies are more appropriate for explosive materials with low vapor pressure, such as military plastic explosives.

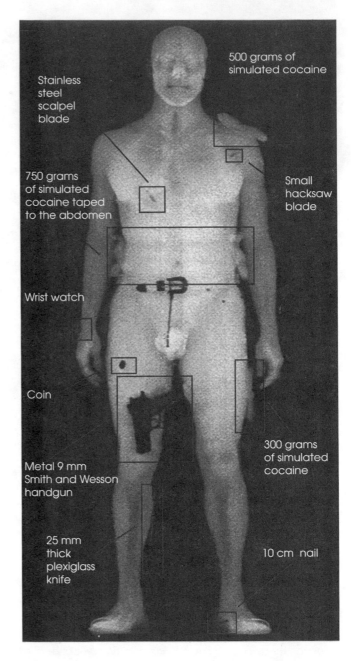

FIGURE 3-6a   Visual image of a person being scanned by the BodySearch 1 produced by AS&E.
FIGURE 3-6b   X-ray image of the same person showing a variety of hidden threat objects, including a Plexiglas knife, a 9mm handgun, and simulated drugs. Reproduced courtesy of AS&E (1995).

Samples can be taken either by having the subject walk through a portal or by passing a hand-wand device over the subject. Either method may be implemented as a *contact* or *noncontact* technique. In contact portal sampling, passengers walk through a portal by pushing open a door or by rubbing against paddles or brushes. In a noncontact system, an air stream passes over the passengers as they walk through the portal. Hand-wand devices may be used to sample air around the person or to make physical contact. In general, contact methods focus on gathering particulates of explosive material from the hands or clothing of the subject. Noncontact methods may use the air stream to dislodge particles, or they may distill a sample of explosive vapor from the air stream.

Although using a hand-wand device is a potentially efficient sample-collection technique, it is more labor intensive and more time consuming than collecting samples using an automated portal. The optimum solution may be to attach a hand-wand device to a portal-based trace-detection system as a higher-level surveillance accessory. This is a common technique used with metal-detection portals. In trace detection, a

TABLE 3-2 Passenger Screening Technologies Based on Trace Detection

Implemented as . . .	Comments
Portal screening—noncontact	Involves high-volume airflow to gather vapors or to dislodge particles from surfaces
Portal screening—contact	Passenger opens *saloon doors* with hands
Portal screening—contact	Passenger passes through a portal lined with brushes or fronds and brushes against them
Hand-wand device—noncontact	Involves high-volume airflow to gather vapors or to dislodge particles adhering to surfaces
Canine screening—noncontact	Technology currently in use
Boarding-card scanner—contact	Boarding card is scanned after handling by passenger for particles of explosive materials

Source: Jankowski (1995a, b).

single chemical-identification instrument could be served by both the portal and the hand-wand device sample-collection mechanisms.

Because it is difficult to extract explosive vapors from large volumes of air or to gather particulates of explosive materials from the great variety of materials on which particles of explosive materials might be found, it is not surprising that no sampling technique that is universally adoptable has been identified. Developers have tried dislodging material mechanically with air-brush and air-vacuum devices. Although every approach is effective under specific sampling conditions, none of the techniques has shown itself universally effective. The lack of a specific sampling approach makes it difficult to discuss a generic *trace* method. It also creates problems in designing a standard testing and certification protocol for comparing the effectiveness of various technological approaches.

A problem in all trace-detection approaches is clearing vapors or particles of explosive materials from the sample-collection mechanism so that subsequent readings are not influenced by previous traces of explosive materials. The baseline readings must be monitored to alert operators to elevated levels of contamination before the contamination results in the shut-down of the equipment.

Identifying Explosive Materials

After a sample is collected, a variety of commercially available chemical-identification technologies may be used to determine if the sample contains any explosive materials. The detection limit of most technologies under consideration by the FAA is generally sufficient to identify explosive materials in a sample. Even average-performance mass spectrometers are capable of measuring and identifying ultra-trace quantities of relevant chemicals, but more highly trained operators may be required to maintain a high level of detection capability. Much of the work sponsored by the FAA in trace-detection technologies concentrates on integrating a particular chemical-identification technique with a sampling technique.

The chemical-identification part of the trace-detection instrument is likely to be smaller than the portal or sample-collection portion of the system. Therefore, for portal-type systems, airport accommodation is generally not dependent on the size of the chemical-identification component of the system but will more likely be affected by how the sample collection is implemented.

Some chemical-identification technologies may be small enough to be incorporated into hand-held instruments and thus have potential use in hand-wand devices. Technologies under consideration include pyroluminescence (for detecting solid particles of explosives, e.g., gun powder), chemical sensors, and ion-drift spectroscopy. As discussed above, these technologies must be combined with a sample-collection technique. The need to move large amounts of air in collecting a sample most likely means that available sample-collection techniques may limit the application of these technologies to continuous surveillance methods relying exclusively on the use of hand-wand devices.

NONIMAGING ELECTROMAGNETIC TECHNOLOGIES

Nonimaging electromagnetic screening technologies are used in places as diverse as libraries, court houses, schools, sports stadiums, and clothing stores. These mature technologies function as metal detectors to deter theft and to ensure safety. For airport use, a potential improvement would be to make these technologies specifically sensitive to weapons. As most travelers know, current metal detectors can be triggered by common, nonthreat objects, such as belt buckles or shoes with metal shanks. Resolving these false alarms consumes time and resources and fosters an air of complacency regarding the detection of real threat objects. Other improvements include making the metal detectors (1) more versatile in detecting a broad spectrum of alloys, (2) more specific in locating suspected threat items, and, (3) more tolerant of electrical noise from nearby sources, such as video display terminals and fluorescent lights. These improvements would probably go unnoticed by passengers and cause little concern to airport management, from the standpoint of increased requirements for utilities and space.

The FAA is also considering a nonimaging dielectric portal designed by Spatial Dynamics Applications, Inc. Discovery systems based on this technique have been used for many years by the U.S. Customs Service to search for contraband in cargo being brought into the United States. This technique uses microwave irradiation and a transmitter/receiver pair to determine the complex dielectric constant of the object being screened. The dielectric constant measured is compared to known responses for humans and threat objects to determine the presence of dangerous items. While the system being developed for consideration by the FAA is based on a simple signal comparison, the same technology could be used to produce an image in a manner similar to the technologies discussed above. For passenger screening, the person being screened steps into a portal and is scanned from head to toe to reveal the presence of both metallic and nonmetallic objects. The levels of microwave power used for weapons discovery are less than 0.1 percent of the levels established by the U.S. Food and Drug Administration (FDA) for microwave energy safety (Burnett et al., 1992). A single 360° scan is completed in approximately four seconds.

Hand-wand electromagnetic screening devices are used for locating specific items that set off alarms in portals and for screening persons who, for one reason or another, cannot or will not pass through portals. These devices, which can be manipulated with one hand, are slower than walk-through portals in screening passengers. The health and safety concerns associated with these devices are minimal, and their widespread use in airports apparently elicits little negative reaction from passengers.

Nonimaging electromagnetic screening technologies are unable to detect nonmetallic objects or materials. Technologies based on microwave irradiation are capable of detecting both metallic and nonmetallic threat objects.

CLEARING AN ALARM

The panel limited the definition of *clearing the alarm* to the equipment itself, that is, returning the instrument to its pre-examination state. The steps taken to determine whether the alarm was set off because dangerous materials or objects

are indeed present are procedural. Therefore, they lie beyond the scope of this report.

Only trace-detection technology is expected to be affected by possible problems related to clearing the alarm. Neither imaging technologies nor nonimaging electromagnetic technologies have a memory effect. Therefore, settings usually return to the baseline state after the subject exits the inspection area. For these technologies, alarms are cleared simply by resetting the equipment to its pre-examination state.

In contrast to imaging technologies and nonimaging electromagnetic technologies, trace-detection equipment interacts with the vapor or particulate form of the materials of interest and signals the presence of these substances when their concentrations are above a threshold level. Ideally, the instrument signal should return automatically to its baseline value once detection has been completed. However, if the area around the sampling inlet is contaminated or if the trace compound lingers in the intake part of the instrument, the equipment will be unable to immediately return its settings to their baseline levels. Lingering *contamination* could result in persistent elevated signals, possibly above the alarm threshold value, and could cause the equipment to continue to indicate the presence of dangerous materials long after the original alarm-triggering event has passed.

Contamination of the intake part of the system may occur (1) if a vapor has high affinity for the material(s) in the sample collection part of the instrument and is present in high concentrations during the subject-screening stage, or (2) if the particulate trace is dislodged from the subject by mechanical means (e.g., an air brush), has high affinity for the sample collection materials, or lodges in the sample collection mechanism and has significant vapor pressure.

For the equipment to be contaminated by the material being detected, all conditions in either scenario 1 or 2 above would have to be satisfied simultaneously. Although these scenarios are unlikely, the probability may be minimized by the judicious choice of the materials used in manufacturing the sample-collection component of the system. The materials should have a low free energy of adsorption for the molecules of the explosive materials the instrument is designed to detect to prevent the molecules from adhering to the inlet walls. As an additional feature, the instrument should be equipped with a mechanism for bypassing the sample collection inlet. This mechanism could be used to provide uncontaminated ambient air to verify the proper operation of the instrument after the identification of explosive materials. These are issues that manufacturers of trace-detection equipment should address.

Aside from dealing with problems related to lingering contamination, manufacturers also have to address the tendency of trace-detection systems to react to the presence of materials, particularly certain medications, that are chemically similar to explosive materials. This tendency leads to *false positives*, which are likely to be more common than the detection of true threat materials, and the need for operators to clear the equipment before being able to proceed with passenger screening.

SUMMARY

The trade-off between technology performance and acceptance by air carriers or the public is a feature common to imaging, nonimaging, and trace-detection technologies. For example, a sharper (i.e., less ambiguous) image could be obtained by increasing observation time, but doing so could add to passenger delays. The intensity of the incident beam could also be increased, but this could lead to increased passenger concerns about exposure to radiation. Similarly, a more aggressive sampling for trace detection could lead to a higher rate of positive identification of explosive materials, at the expense of making the sample-collection phase more personally invasive to the passenger. Ultimately, the performance capability and quality of a passenger screening technology is unlikely to be the limiting factor in its implementation or application. Limitations on the technology will instead be imposed as a result of passenger intolerance for invasion of privacy, delays, or discomfort.

4

Operational and Cost Issues

Air carriers are responsible for maintaining air travel security. Part of this responsibility entails developing and using a security program that includes screening all passengers. Operationally, this responsibility means that air carriers purchase equipment, design and set up checkpoints covering access to their outbound flights, and hire and train personnel to operate these checkpoints. The costs associated with this security-screening program include both the security-screening equipment and the personnel to operate the equipment and to resolve alarms.

AIR CARRIER OPERATIONS

For air carriers, quick and inexpensive screening of passengers and carry-on baggage is a major concern. Based on estimates of traveler loads throughout the day at a particular airport, air carriers must purchase and deploy an optimum number of screening devices and screening personnel. Air carriers often hire independent firms to operate security checkpoints. These firms provide both equipment and personnel, but the ultimate responsibility for security screening remains with the air carriers.

The panel believes new security-screening equipment based on the technologies discussed in this report will be more expensive to purchase than current screening equipment. However, each new technology offers additional capabilities over present screening technologies. Increased costs may be offset or justified if, for example, new equipment requires fewer checkpoints or if fewer personnel can operate the new equipment and resolve alarms. The issue of the cost of implementing new aviation security measures is complicated and involves much more than the cost of the new equipment.

Of course, the new technologies are likely to offer a higher level of security because of their ability to detect a wider variety of threat objects or to target threat objects more specifically. However, in discussing the costs of security screening, it is difficult to estimate the value of a higher level of security. While the panel believes that airport security can, and should, be improved, the appropriate timetable for incorporating new technology into security checkpoints of the future will depend greatly on the perceived level of threat and on the evaluation of all costs associated with the implementation of a given technology.

AIRPORT FACILITIES OPERATIONS

Operators of airport facilities are also charged with developing and implementing security procedures. The goal of airport operators is to provide a secure environment in which air carriers can operate. This includes offering law enforcement support to air carriers when threat objects are identified through passenger screening procedures.

Airport operators are most interested and concerned with the space requirements of safety and security programs instituted at airports. The space requirement issue encompasses the physical area required to set up or establish a security checkpoint and the area required for the queuing up passengers or baggage. Unusual power requirements or nonstandard equipment needs, such as liquid nitrogen, are also of concern to airport operators. Facility space requirements involve more than simply square footage. Both the three-dimensional volume and the weight of each piece of equipment must be included in the equation for determining the space needed and other location requirements for establishing a screening checkpoint.

Newer designs for airport terminals have taken into account the requirements of passenger screening operations, based on the best estimates of the demands for equipment and operational space and for the queuing space required for projected passenger loads. Equipment and operational space is determined by the number of checkpoints and the size of the equipment the air carrier wishes to install. Queuing space is directly linked to projected passenger traffic, which depends on the size of the aircraft and the number of flights anticipated by the air carrier.

Older airport facilities designed and built before hub operations or passenger screening are often strained to meet current space requirements, especially when changes in operational procedures require additional equipment for each passenger screening point. An example of the effect of procedural changes on space requirements is the need of some air carriers for additional space for a second metal-detector portal for screening passengers who trigger the alarm at the first metal-detector portal.

DELAYS CAUSED BY AVIATION SECURITY MEASURES

One of the biggest costs associated with aviation security is the delay imposed on travelers and air carriers. Often, arriving at the airport 15 minutes before departure may be enough for domestic flights. However, air travel becomes significantly less convenient and more expensive, in terms of direct costs to business travelers, when passengers have to arrive earlier at the airport to accommodate additional passenger screening procedures. This is especially true during high threat situations when passengers may be required to arrive at least two hours early.

Domestic air travel requires an efficient system of carefully scheduled connecting flights and short aircraft ground time. If a flight is delayed, air carriers incur significant costs in rescheduling passengers who miss connecting flights. For international air travel, delays cause fewer problems because many of the passengers begin and end their travel on one flight. International travelers also are likely to arrive well in advance of their scheduled departure time.

The level of security (and the potential length of delay incurred) should be commensurate with the threat. However, a basic level of security still must be maintained, even if no specific threat is apparent. The time needed for security screening causes delays. Security screening is accomplished through a serial inspection process, but when the queues grow long, a second process may be set up parallel to the first. In practice, the amount of security equipment and the number of personnel required can vary significantly over time. If a high threat situation occurs when only normal security equipment and personnel are available, then significant delays will result. Using computer simulations to estimate the time required for intensified security inspections during high threat situations is the best way to determine the length of delays and the probable effects. The FAA is working on providing this type of simulation capability to air carriers, and the panel recommends the continuation of this work, in parallel with the development of new technologies for passenger screening.

SUMMARY

Air carriers and airport authorities are concerned with the cost of new technologies, although each emphasizes a different aspect of the cost. Air carriers bear the cost of the equipment and the personnel to operate it; they also bear the cost of delays incurred when security screening interrupts the orderly flow of flights. Airport facility operators are responsible for providing appropriate space and other building requirements.

Before implementing new security-screening technologies, both airport operators and air carriers will demand well-supported data showing that the new technologies will add significantly to existing security-screening capabilities. Airports and air carriers will also have to consider carefully whether the new technologies will offset added costs for new equipment by lowering costs for other factors, such as the number of personnel or checkpoints.

5

Operator Ergonomics, Selection, Training, and Motivation

Poor operator performance is a principal weakness of existing passenger screening systems and a potential weakness of future systems (Fobes, 1995). Currently, personnel at screening checkpoints are required to perform tasks for which human beings are not well suited. These tasks are performed under conditions that degrade whatever performance capabilities they do have and for wages that may be competitive only with entry-level wages in the fast-food industry. The screener of carry-on baggage, for example, is required to identify sometimes faint indications of infrequently appearing target items. These objects may take an almost infinite number of shapes and orientations in a wide variety of baggage types. An abundance of research on tasks requiring signal detection under conditions of sustained attention confirms that acceptable levels of performance on such tasks are difficult to achieve, even under the best working conditions (Davies and Parasuraman, 1982; Mackie, 1987).

The conditions under which these tasks are performed at airport screening checkpoints are likely to degrade low performance levels even further. In a recent survey of passenger screening personnel, the top five problems identified by respondents all related to the abuse of screening personnel by passengers, air carrier personnel, and others (Dennison, 1995). The low pay and stressful working conditions lead to a high and costly rate of employee turnover. A large provider of passenger screening services reported that the company hired 20,000 people in 1994 to staff 8,000 screening positions (Dennison, 1995).

The successful implementation of a passenger screening method or system requires a program of laboratory and field research to address issues regarding the effectiveness of screening operators. This chapter addresses implementation issues that involve (1) the performance of system operators, (2) the application of the principles of ergonomics[1] in the design of screening systems, and (3) the selection, training, and motivation of system operators.

RELATIONSHIP BETWEEN PAY AND PERFORMANCE

The low wages currently paid to operators of passenger- and baggage-screening systems has been raised frequently as an issue related to poor operator performance. An explicit or implicit assumption is that higher wages will attract *better* people to these jobs, which, in turn, will lead to better operator performance. However, increased pay alone is not likely to improve operator performance significantly. A substantial body of evidence suggests that any direct link between pay and performance is tenuous at best and is probably insignificant compared to more powerful determinants of operator performance (Guzzo, 1988; Guzzo et al., 1985; Hertzberg, 1968; Lawler, 1971, 1981). The best result that can be expected from higher wages is less turnover among operators (a severe problem in itself), which could lead to opportunities to implement better selection, training, and motivation methods.

Because the lack of a relationship between higher pay and better performance is counterintuitive, figure 5-1 and the following discussion are offered as a simplified framework for understanding this relationship. Figure 5-1 also serves as a structure for understanding why operator ergonomics, selection, training, and motivation must be addressed in combination in order to enhance job performance. Based on the summaries of research findings referenced above, figure 5-1 shows that attaining job effectiveness involves the application of two types of factors—those that attract and keep people on the job (maintenance factors) and those that lead to acceptable or enhanced performance on the job (performance factors).

Maintenance factors attract people to jobs and keep them on the job long enough to permit performance factors to operate. As shown in figure 5-1, compensation (wages and benefits) is only one of several maintenance factors and, as a consequence, it is indirectly related to performance. Higher levels of some factors can compensate for lower levels of other factors in providing a sufficiently attractive combination to keep a person on the job. For example, higher levels of pay might make up for poor working conditions or the low status of the job or organization.

Performance factors lead to acceptable levels of job performance or serve as avenues for enhancing performance beyond existing levels. One of the most important and powerful of these factors is the design of the job or task. As

---

[1]Ergonomics refers to the design of systems in such a way that their operational requirements are compatible with the human capabilities and limitations of their operators.

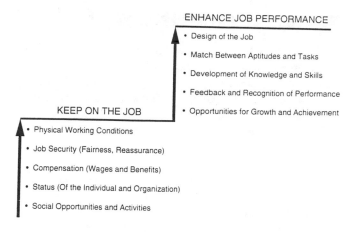

ENHANCE JOB PERFORMANCE

• Design of the Job

• Match Between Aptitudes and Tasks

• Development of Knowledge and Skills

• Feedback and Recognition of Performance

• Opportunities for Growth and Achievement

KEEP ON THE JOB

• Physical Working Conditions

• Job Security (Fairness, Reassurance)

• Compensation (Wages and Benefits)

• Status (Of the Individual and Organization)

• Social Opportunities and Activities

FIGURE 5-1 Factors that influence job performance.

discussed earlier, performance is greatly influenced by the extent to which the job and task requirements are compatible with the capabilities and limitations of the employee. The objective of ergonomics is to assure this compatibility. Another important factor, particularly in light of the seemingly large individual differences in aptitudes among screening personnel, is the match between the aptitudes of the employee and the skill requirements of the job. This match is a function of the procedures employed for selecting and assigning personnel to specific jobs. Also, to the extent to which they can be incorporated into the job, recognition of performance, opportunities for feelings of achievement, and opportunities for growth can serve to enhance performance. An example of an opportunity for growth was given by D. Issacharoff of El Al Airlines in his presentation to the panel. He told the panel that personnel hired by the company that performs passenger screening for El Al Airlines are given the opportunity to advance to jobs with the airline. In the United States, passenger screening personnel are often employees of a contractor company, and, generally, they do not have the opportunity to advance beyond a supervisory role at security checkpoints.

Thus, the relationship between pay and performance is an indirect one. Adequate pay provides a foundation for realizing adequate or enhanced levels of performance, but a combination of performance factors must be present as well. For example, if the effectiveness of a passenger screening system depends on certain operator aptitudes, then increased wages will not result in increased levels of performance, if the employee does not have these aptitudes to begin with.

ERGONOMICS IN SYSTEM DESIGN

According to data provided by the FAA (1995), operator performance in conducting passenger screening using current systems and procedures is not uniformly effective. Applying the principles of ergonomics in the design of screening systems and procedures is a possible avenue to improving the performance of current and future systems. The allocation of functions between machine and operator, in particular, will have a significant influence on the effectiveness of future systems. This allocation will dictate the specific tasks to be performed by the operator and the manner in which the operator must perform them. The goal is to ensure that functions assigned to humans are compatible with human capabilities. If they are not, then assigned functions will not be performed well, even if the best personnel selection, training, and motivation approaches are employed.

The resolution of issues related to ergonomics will be critical to the success of new passenger screening systems. In an apparent paradox, as screening systems become more automated, human factors are likely to become even more critical to success. Human operators will perform the difficult and complex tasks that cannot be automated. Increased automation will also introduce a host of new human factors issues that must be addressed (see, for example, Rasmussen, 1986; Wiener, 1987; Reason, 1990). One such issue deals with effectively integrating available information for screening and alarm resolution decisions. Which of the variety of techniques available for use in data integration and display will be most effective for passenger screening? Another issue will be the design of calibration, testing, and maintenance systems that are likely to be more complex for more highly automated systems.

Ergonomics issues can be addressed by applying existing knowledge, by conducting research in laboratory and field settings, and by incorporating appropriate measures in system test and evaluation programs. To realize the benefits of these efforts for any specific system, however, these issues must be integrated into the system development process. The FAA can ensure that system developers address critical human factors issues by incorporating appropriate and sufficiently sensitive measures of human performance in suitable system test protocols. These test protocols must be designed and employed to evaluate and qualify systems prior to their implementation, and they should be specified in advance to system developers.

The importance of ergonomics in system effectiveness is illustrated by the inadequate design of existing systems. Current systems for screening carry-on baggage continue to suffer from human factors issues that were not and have not been addressed properly. In an example cited by a workshop participant, the effectiveness of current screening systems can be jeopardized by pressures imposed by management on operators to increase the rate of passenger screening (Dennison, 1995). Other data from the FAA show that the overall detection effectiveness of existing human-machine screening systems is lower than desirable (FAA, 1995). According to an official of one of the largest providers of screening services in the United States, examples of inadequacies in existing baggage-screening systems include the following (Dennison, 1995):

- The display does not provide the operator with adequate size reference (i.e., all bags, regardless of size, appear about the same size on the screen).
- Equipment controls are insufficiently distinguishable by shape and location coding to permit operation without looking at the control panel.
- Data integration and image-processing techniques have not been sufficiently exploited to provide enhancements for image interpretation.
- Equipment design forces operators to position themselves improperly to view the display.
- Work force constraints (e.g., the requirement to rotate personnel among all positions at specified time intervals) limit the ability of management to assign security personnel to tasks in accordance with their abilities.
- Passengers, airport staff, air carrier employees, and others sometimes subject security personnel to abuse.

Important steps have been taken by the FAA to ensure that critical and high-priority issues related to the enhancement of operator performance in security systems are addressed systematically. The FAA has initiated a program of ergonomics research and development that parallels, and is integrated with, the development of new technologies and systems. The human factors program should remain a high priority for the general FAA aviation security program because operator performance is important to the overall effectiveness of security systems. In addition, improvements in operator performance can result in immediate improvements in the passenger screening systems themselves.

OPERATOR SELECTION, TRAINING, AND MOTIVATION

To complement the effective design of systems and procedures and to assure acceptable levels of operator performance, the following steps are required for developing personnel selection, training, and motivation methods:

- Develop and apply selection methods to ensure that operators have the necessary aptitudes for the tasks to be performed.
- Develop and administer training systems that provide operators with the needed knowledge and skills.
- Incorporate elements into the system (e.g., ongoing performance measurement and assessment procedures) that enhance rather than degrade operator motivation and job satisfaction.

MEASURING OPERATOR PERFORMANCE

A critical element of an effective program of operator ergonomics, selection, training, and motivation is a set of techniques for measuring operator performance. Measurement will also help the FAA and air carriers to determine the effectiveness of current and future screening systems. The following are some areas that require performance measurement methods:

- assessment of the effect of prototype screening systems, equipment, and procedures on operator performance
- development of criteria for validating operator selection and placement methods
- development of criteria for evaluating the effectiveness of operator training techniques, methods, and programs
- on-line monitoring and evaluation of the effectiveness of security screening systems and personnel
- provision of feedback to individual operators on overall performance and diagnoses of weaknesses

The FAA has initiated a promising research and development program that will lead to the development of techniques for measuring operator performance. These techniques include provisions for electronically inserting target objects in operational screening systems. This program, initiated in 1991, is a focus of the FAA human factors program in 1996.

POTENTIAL OPERATOR CONCERNS WITH SPECIFIC SCREENING TECHNOLOGIES

Imaging Technologies

Imaging technologies produce images of individuals and objects concealed under clothing. Operators are required to interpret images using current imaging technologies. Therefore, the methods used for selecting, training, and motivating operators should be similar to those used for preparing operators of current x-ray baggage-screening equipment. The time available for an operator to decide whether an individual should be allowed to pass or should be held for further screening is short, perhaps no more than six seconds. This is the approximate time currently required for clearing a carry-on bag through the screening equipment. The short time available emphasizes the importance of proper operator selection and training in obtaining and interpreting images.

For imaging technologies, alarm resolution probably will involve either taking additional images (e.g., from different angles) or having a more experienced viewer or supervisor interpret the initial image. Alarm resolution may not require more skill than that required for interpreting the initial image. In fact, the decision to screen a passenger further could result in more time for image interpretation and could offer a chance for less experienced screeners to practice image interpretation.

Trace-Detection Technologies

The use of trace-detection technologies in passenger screening settings may involve person-to-person contact or direct contact between the detection equipment (e.g., trace-chemical sensor) and an individual. As with current screening techniques, operators may feel intimidated by some people they are required to screen. Technologies that require even closer interaction between the operator and the passenger are likely to exacerbate this problem.

Automated trace-detection technologies, where a person is brushed with an air stream or is required to touch a portion of the equipment, do not impose additional requirements on operators. As in current passenger screening techniques, operators generally will become involved only after an alarm is triggered. More skilled operators are required for maintaining sophisticated chemical-identification systems in acceptable operating condition than for current airport checkpoints.

Nonimaging Electromagnetic Technologies

Changes in these passenger screening devices, including improvements to current technologies and the development of new approaches, are likely to be transparent to both passengers and operators. Security-screening operators will benefit from technologies that will allow them to quickly identify the item that caused the alarm by providing them better information about the type and location of the item.

SUMMARY

Ensuring the satisfactory performance of system operators involves applying ergonomics in the design of screening systems and in developing effective techniques and procedures for selecting, training, and motivating system operators. The resolution of ergonomics issues will enhance the capabilities of current technologies and will be critical to the successful implementation of new passenger screening systems. Improved personnel selection, training, and motivation methods will complement the effective design of systems and procedures and will assure acceptable levels of operator performance. The human factors program of the FAA is a key effort in improving operator performance.

6

Health Effects

Exposure to radiation and to electric and magnetic fields associated with passenger screening devices are not expected to cause adverse health effects in passengers. Radiation levels used by the technologies under consideration in this report are far below the levels that have been linked to health effects. The level of ionizing radiation[1] in passenger screening technologies is compared to the levels of exposure to ionizing radiation from other sources in figure 6-1. Low-energy electromagnetic radiation includes radio waves, microwaves, radar, and power-frequency radiation from electric and magnetic fields associated with electric currents. (See figure 3-1 for the different wavelengths and frequencies of the components of the electromagnetic spectrum.) Passenger screening devices operate using radiation and electric- and magnetic-field levels well below the maximum allowable exposure levels established to protect public health. The health effects of theoretical concern in passenger screening include cancer, reproductive and teratogenic effects, and cardiac effects in passengers with pacemakers.

CANCER

Cancer is the second leading cause of death in the United States. Approximately 1.25 million new cases (excluding skin cancer) are diagnosed each year, and cancer accounts for 550,000 (or one out of five) deaths annually. The major causes of cancer are tobacco use and dietary factors. It is known that various external factors (e.g., tobacco, viruses, and radiation) and internal or host factors (e.g., hormones, immune status, and genetic factors) can combine or interact sequentially to initiate and promote carcinogenesis and to facilitate tumor growth (American Cancer Society, 1995; Doll and Peto, 1981).

Ionizing Radiation

With the possible exception of cigarette smoking, ionizing radiation is probably the most thoroughly studied human

carcinogen. We know more about the cancer-causing effects of ionizing radiation than about most other known or suspected human carcinogens. Ionizing radiation is less carcinogenic than other known human carcinogens, and it is responsible for only a small part of the cancer burden in the United States. Less than 5 percent of all cancer deaths may be attributable to exposure to ionizing radiation. The principal sources of radiation exposure to the U.S. population are the natural radiation background and medical and dental radiodiagnostic procedures. The primary factors contributing to cancer are tobacco consumption and dietary habits. Together, these two causes account for about two-thirds of all cancer deaths (Doll and Peto, 1981).

Evidence of ionizing radiation as a human carcinogen is derived from a number of epidemiological studies involving exposures of human populations from the military, medical, and occupational uses of radiation. Such evidence is derived almost exclusively from epidemiological studies of populations exposed to high doses of radiation. Radiation-induced cancer has not been observed in populations exposed to radiation doses of less than 10 to 20 rem (0.1 to 0.2 Sv).[2] The single most important study involves the long-term evaluation of the Japanese survivors of the atomic bombings of Hiroshima and Nagasaki in 1945. In the Life Span Study (one of several cohort-based epidemiological studies) conducted by the Radiation Effects Research Foundation, more than 75,000 atomic bomb survivors are being studied. Mortality rates and causes of death are continuously updated. Individuals in the study received doses ranging from less than 10 rem (0.1 Sv) to more than 500 rem (5 Sv). The average dose to survivors of the bombings was approximately 20 rem (0.2 Sv). In the mortality survey from 1950 to 1985, a total of 6,000 cancer deaths have been observed; only about 350 excess cancers that have been observed to date could be attributable to radiation exposure (NRC, 1990; UNSCEAR, 1994).

Epidemiological studies have also been conducted to evaluate the health effects of exposure to natural background radiation. Individuals in the United States are exposed to 200

---

[1] In the context of this report, ionizing radiation is defined as high-energy electromagnetic radiation capable of disrupting chemical bonds and causing biological injury through the process of ionization. Ultraviolet light, visible light, and radio waves are examples of lower energy electromagnetic radiation that interacts with matter and causes biological damage by other mechanisms.

These types of radiation are referred to in this report as nonionizing radiation.

[2] Rem is a measure of the effect of radiation on the human body. It takes into account both the amount of radiation deposited in body tissues and the type of radiation. A millirem is one-thousandth of a rem. A newer unit is the sievert (Sv). 1 Sv = 100 rem.

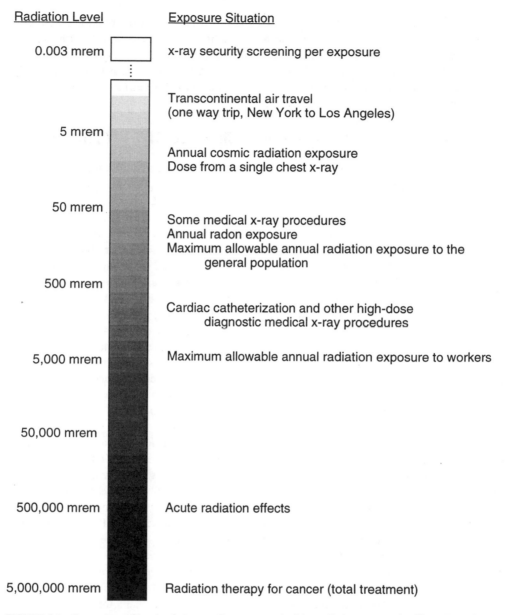

Radiation Level   **Exposure Situation**

0.003 mrem — x-ray security screening per exposure

Transcontinental air travel
(one way trip, New York to Los Angeles)

5 mrem — Annual cosmic radiation exposure
Dose from a single chest x-ray

50 mrem — Some medical x-ray procedures
Annual radon exposure
Maximum allowable annual radiation exposure to the
    general population

500 mrem — Cardiac catheterization and other high-dose
    diagnostic medical x-ray procedures

5,000 mrem — Maximum allowable annual radiation exposure to workers

50,000 mrem

500,000 mrem — Acute radiation effects

5,000,000 mrem — Radiation therapy for cancer (total treatment)

FIGURE 6-1 Comparison of levels of exposure from common ionizing radiation sources (1 millirem [mrem] = 0.01 millisievert [mSv]). Sources: NCRP (1987) and Nicolet Imaging Systems (1995).

to 300 millirem (2 to 3 mSv) annually from natural background radiation, including radioactive materials from the earth's crust and cosmic rays from outer space (NRC, 1990). No evidence has been found of an increase in cancer or other diseases among people living in areas where natural background radiation is several times higher than average (up to 500 to 600 millirem [5 to 6 mSv] per year), such as in Han, China; Kerala, India; or Araxa-Tapira, Brazil (NCRP, 1987; NRC, 1990).

Although no epidemiological studies have shown conclusively that ionizing radiation at low doses (less than 10 rem [0.1 Sv]) causes cancer, it is nevertheless assumed that low doses of radiation are carcinogenic. A popular view within the scientific community is expressed through the linear no-threshold model, which assumes that the risk of developing cancer is directly proportional to dose, even at very low doses, and that any dose, no matter how small, may be damaging. Dose extrapolation under this or other dose-response models must be viewed with caution. First, there is a paucity of data in the low-dose region. Thus, large uncertainties exist for estimates of health effects at low doses. Second, the extrapolation process, especially for the well known linear no-threshold model, assumes that carcinogenic mechanisms operative at high dose levels are also relevant at low dose levels. This assumption is probably not valid because significant cell killing, which occurs in the high-dose range (doses above 100 rem [1 Sv]), probably occurs to a much smaller degree, if at all, at low dose levels. Cell killing may play an important role in carcinogenesis by promoting cell division in surviving cells. Furthermore, the body is capable of repairing radiation damage in cells, and damage would be more likely repaired at low doses.

Linear extrapolation to very low doses is often without practical meaning. Although it is theoretically possible that a small exposure might result in a cancer, the probability at very low doses is vanishingly small and on the order of one in a billion. For example, if one airport screening with an x-ray imaging device results in 0.003 mrem (0.00003 mSv) (Smith 1995), and if the lifetime probability of cancer mortality is 1 in 1,000,000 per mrem (per 0.01 mSv) (UNSCEAR 1994), then the theoretical risk associated with cancer mortality from a single screen approaches 3 in 1 billion. Considering that the lifetime cancer mortality rate for Americans from all causes is about 20 percent (or 1 in 5), these small probabilities are practically meaningless.

Nonionizing Radiation

Compared to ionizing radiation, much less evidence exists that nonionizing fields, such as extremely low-frequency (e.g., 60 Hz [cycles per second]) electric and magnetic fields, cause cancer. Although some epidemiological studies suggest statistical associations of this type of radiation with cancer (primarily childhood leukemia), others do not, and experimental studies have not yielded reproducible evidence of carcinogenic mechanisms (ORAU, 1992; American Cancer Society, 1995). The above statements apply to both transient fields, such as those being considered for future passenger screening technologies, and quasi-static fields, such as those found near power lines.

Although laboratory studies have confirmed that low levels of electromagnetic radiation may cause biochemical and physiological changes in cells, they do not appear to damage DNA directly, and, therefore, would be unlikely to initiate cancer. Cancer was first associated epidemiologically with exposure to low-frequency electromagnetic fields in 1979 when a higher-than-expected occurrence of leukemia was reported in children residing in homes adjacent to high-current power lines (Wertheimer and Leeper, 1979). Since this initial report, a number of other studies have shown statistical associations between cancer and exposure to various sources of electromagnetic fields. However, these epidemiological studies have been difficult to interpret because of various inadequacies in experimental design, including the lack of individual exposure measurements and incomplete consideration of confounding factors. Accordingly, a causal relation between electromagnetic-field exposure and cancer has not been established (NRPB, 1992; ORAU, 1992).

Recent studies of childhood brain cancer and of electrical utility workers provide little or no support for the hypothesis that low-frequency electromagnetic field exposures (60 Hz) represent a health hazard (Kheifets et al., 1995; Preston-Martin et al., 1996; Gurney et al. 1996).

REPRODUCTIVE HEALTH EFFECTS

The U.S. Bureau of the Census estimates that there are 6.3 million pregnancies[3] each year in the United States (U.S. Bureau of the Census, 1994). Developing human embryos or fetuses are subject to risks from a spectrum of effects, including mental retardation and malformations, from relatively high doses of ionizing radiation that pose no risks to adults. This enhanced sensitivity to radiation is due to the high rate of cellular proliferation and differentiation during fetal life. Damage to a single embryonic cell may be multiplied enormously during growth and development. Enhanced sensitivity is not restricted to radiation; exposures to various chemical and biological agents may also be associated with increased reproductive risks. For instance, a higher incidence of adverse pregnancy outcomes, such as intrauterine growth retardation, occurs in women with a history of smoking and chronic alcohol consumption during pregnancy (Mossman and Hill, 1982).

Screening devices based on exposure to electromagnetic radiation or magnetic fields are common in everyday situations, such as in libraries and stores. Passenger screening devices based on these technologies involve exposure at insignificant levels compared to radiation levels from other commonly accepted radiation sources (such as those shown in figure 6-1). Thus, these technologies are not expected to cause adverse health effects to developing embryos or fetuses. At much higher doses, ionizing radiation is known to cause developmental effects in humans. Furthermore, substantial evidence exists that a threshold dose of 10 to 20 rem (0.1 to 0.2 Sv) must be exceeded in order to produce prenatal effects, such as developmental anomalies and mental retardation. Significant adverse pregnancy outcomes, such as birth defects and spontaneous abortions, have been observed in cases where the fetus has been given doses in excess of several hundred rem (several Sv) (Brent, 1980). Radiation doses to passengers undergoing x-ray screening are many orders of magnitude below these thresholds and much lower than doses from exposure to natural background radiation or even doses from the cosmic ray exposure during a transcontinental flight.

Epidemiological studies have not been conducted to evaluate directly the reproductive risks of exposure to screening

---

[3]This was the total number of pregnancies in 1988 (the most recent data available). Pregnancies include live births (3.9 million) and induced abortions and fetal losses (2.4 million).

devices considered in this report. However, a large number of epidemiological studies have been conducted on reproductive and teratogenic effects (e.g., birth defects and spontaneous abortions) in human population groups exposed to electromagnetic and magnetic fields from video display terminals (VDTs), power lines, and household appliances (ORAU, 1992). The results of these studies strongly suggest that the radiation and field exposures at levels associated with passenger screening devices do not have reproductive or teratogenic effects.

No statistically significant associations have been found in epidemiological studies involving VDTs, which typically expose the operator to maximum magnetic fields of about 2 milligauss (mG)[4] at 30 cm from the screen. This figure is comparable to magnetic fields found near home television sets. A magnetic field strength of 2 mG produces an electric field (at 16,000 Hz) of about 1 millivolt per meter in the abdomen of the operator. For comparison, flying in an airplane through the magnetic field of the earth produces a uniform static electric field of about 10 millivolts per meter through the entire body. In an analysis of 21 epidemiological studies, the overall results indicate that pregnant women exposed to VDTs do not have an increased risk of reproductive defects (ORAU, 1992). The reproductive parameters evaluated in these studies included birth defects, spontaneous abortions, stillbirths, and intrauterine growth retardation (ORAU, 1992).

Fewer epidemiological studies have been conducted on the reproductive risks of exposure to power lines, electric substations, and home appliances. These studies have been difficult to analyze because radiation or field exposures rarely have been determined, and studies frequently involve small sample sizes. Magnetic fields for some common household appliances, such as coffee makers, stereos, refrigerators, and toasters, vary considerably; at 30 cm from the source, the measured magnetic field may vary from 0.1 to 10 mG. House wiring produces a background measured magnetic field of 1 mG or less. In an analysis of five epidemiological studies of various sources of electromagnetic radiation, no statistically significant increase in spontaneous abortions, birth defects, or fetal growth retardation was observed (ORAU, 1992).

HEART DISEASE AND PACEMAKERS

Individuals with cardiac arrhythmia may be fitted with an artificial pacemaker, which emits a series of rhythmic electrical discharges to control the heart rate. It has been estimated that there are over 500,000 patients with pacemakers in the United States; over 100,000 pacemaker procedures are performed annually (American Heart Association, 1995). The effects of radiation-producing equipment on pacemakers vary from no effect to the theoretical possibility of rendering the pacemaker nonfunctional, leading to possible fatal cardiac arrhythmias.

As shown in figure 6-1, passenger screening devices involve exposures to insignificant levels of electromagnetic radiation or magnetic fields. Accordingly, these devices will not produce radiation at levels high enough to damage pacemaker circuitry, cause heat damage, or affect normal pacemaker operation through electromagnetic interference. Certain medical procedures expose patients to radiation levels substantially higher than those used in screening, and these procedures can cause such effects on pacemakers (Hardage et al., 1985).

SOME POSSIBLE HEALTH CONCERNS ASSOCIATED WITH SPECIFIC SCREENING TECHNOLOGIES

Imaging Technologies

Imaging technologies generally involve the use of ionizing radiation (e.g., x-rays) to produce images of individuals and objects that may be concealed under layers of clothing. The images are produced using computer analysis of either reflected, absorbed, or scattered radiation (active imaging), or of natural radiation emitted from the human body (passive imaging). For active imaging, small doses of radiation are used in the imaging process. The level of exposure to x-rays in passenger screening is orders of magnitude below the x-ray levels used in medical diagnosis and represents a fraction of 1 percent of the natural background to which the U.S. population is exposed annually (see figure 6-1). For example, in screening devices using backscatter x-ray, exposures are approximately 0.003 millirem (0.00003 mSv) per individual (Smith, 1995). This radiation level is so low that a passenger would have to go through the screening portal approximately 1,000 times to receive the same radiation dose as would be received from cosmic ray exposure at high altitude during one transcontinental flight from New York to Los Angeles.

Passengers who wear pacemakers are not at additional risk from radiation exposure in passenger screening. Pacemaker malfunction may occur when radiation doses exceed 1,000 rad (10 Gy; for x-rays, 1 rad = 1 rem),[5] as in the case of patients undergoing radiotherapy for cancer, where pacemaker circuitry may fail as a result of radiation damage to the semiconductor circuitry. Function is not affected by x-ray

---

[4]Magnetic flux density is measured in gauss or tesla. A milligauss (mG) is one thousandth of a gauss. The earth's magnetic flux density at the surface due to current flow in the earth's core ranges from 300 to 700 mG (30 to 70 microtesla). The earth's field is a direct magnetic field and not an alternating one, such as the field from electric power transmission lines and appliances. Everyone is exposed to the magnetic flux density of the earth (NRPB, 1992).

[5]The unit of absorbed dose is the rad. One rad is equal to the deposition of 100 ergs of ionizing radiation energy per gram of absorbing substance. A newer is the gray (Gy). 1 Gy=100 rad.

irradiation at doses below about 200 rad (2 Gy) (Hardage et al., 1985).

Trace-Detection Technologies

Trace-detection technologies for passenger screening may involve person-to-person contact or direct contact between the detection equipment (e.g., trace-chemical sensors) and individuals. Personal contact may be a vehicle for transmitting various microbial diseases (bacterial, fungal, and viral in origin) from one individual to another.

Diseases may be transmitted through the inhalation or ingestion of disease-causing microorganisms, direct contact with individuals, or through wounds and cuts. Diseases also may be transmitted through person-to-person contact or when a passenger's hands touch trace-detection equipment. If the transfer of infectious diseases in the passenger screening setting were to occur, it would most likely result from the hand-mediated transfer of disease-producing microorganisms. The hands can infect other areas of the body through direct contact with the nose, mouth, or minor skin wounds. The hands themselves can easily become contaminated through contact with the nose, mouth, areas of skin infection, or the anal region. Intestinal pathogens such as *shigella dysenteriae* can contaminate hands through toilet tissue. Pathogens on the hands can contaminate inanimate objects, such as doorknobs, chairs, and towels, which can then transmit infection.

The likelihood of disease transmission during passenger screening is dependent upon numerous disease-specific factors, including the integrity of the skin and other host factors, the virulence of the disease-causing microorganism, and the number of microorganisms transmitted. The probability of transmitting disease as a consequence of using trace-detection technologies appear insignificant in comparison to other more common disease-transmission scenarios, such as using public washroom facilities.

Cleanliness, both for personnel at the checkpoint and for the passenger screening equipment, is important to prevent the spread of infection when contact is required between people or between a person and a piece of equipment. Hand washing, a fairly simple procedure, can physically remove microorganisms. Washing hands in plain water removes viruses that cause colds (Nester et al., 1995). Equipment should be designed to allow frequent cleaning to minimize disease transmission from passenger to passenger.

Nonimaging Electromagnetic Technologies

Passenger screening devices, such as portal metal detectors, millimeter-wave devices, hand-wand devices, and dielectrometers, utilize nonionizing radiation and low-frequency electric and magnetic fields for detection. The interaction between tissues and the radiation of photon energies lower than ultraviolet (UV) and electric and magnetic fields are complex. These interactions also are markedly different from damage mechanisms associated with x-rays and other forms of ionizing radiation. Measuring energy deposition and field intensities within the body can be difficult (ORAU, 1992).

Many of the biological effects of exposure to electromagnetic fields are well understood and consistent with established mechanisms of physical interaction with tissues. These include effects on perception processes associated with the accumulation and redistribution of electric charge on the surface of the body, effects on electrically excitable tissues such as nerve and muscle tissues, and effects caused by heating tissues. Acute effects and their dependence on the frequency and magnitude of the fields can be predicted from human and experimental animal studies. These acute health effects studies, together with the application of appropriate safety margins, form the basis for establishing international exposure guidelines. A relatively small number of people are likely to be exposed to radiation at levels high enough to cause acute effects. These high radiation levels are generally encountered only in certain medical therapy settings, where exposures are strictly controlled, or in specific occupational settings (NRPB, 1992).

Passenger screening devices emit very low levels of radiation and electric and magnetic fields. No epidemiological studies have been conducted to evaluate the health effects of portal metal detectors and other passenger screening devices. However, available data from epidemiological studies involving comparable radiation and field exposures from other sources suggest that these devices do not pose health risks. For the technologies based on microwave irradiation, the levels of microwave energy that a person being screened would be subject to have been measured to be less than 0.001 times the energy level set by the FDA for emission from microwave ovens (Burnett et al., 1992; Microwave Cooking Handbook, n.d.).

Passengers with pacemakers are not at additional risk from nonionizing radiation and electric and magnetic field exposures from passenger screening. Pacemakers are designed to eliminate electromagnetic interference. Medical therapy devices that operate at much higher energy levels, such as hyperthermia and diathermy units, can cause pacemakers to malfunction by causing permanent damage to pulse generators or temporary changes or total inhibition of the pacing rate (Hardage et al., 1985).

SUMMARY

Radiation for electromagnetic fields from passenger screening devices does not harm the individuals undergoing screening or operating the equipment. Measured radiation levels and electromagnetic fields from these devices are very low and are well below the levels known to have harmful effects.

The panel has determined that the health issue is primarily a *perception of risk* rather than an actual health threat. Concerns about health effects may still affect public acceptance of imaging and nonimaging electromagnetic radiation technologies, especially because people distinguish between radiation received voluntarily (such as radiation during a transcontinental flight) and radiation received involuntarily (such as radiation from living in areas built over piles of uranium mill tailings). People may perceive the radiation they receive to facilitate aviation security as an involuntary dose of radiation that they are unwilling to be exposed to. For example, x-ray screening technologies do not pose a health problem, but people may believe that they do. Therefore, people may object to a technology that exposes them to x-rays, even though the radiation dose is extremely small. This perception may be true especially for aircrews and airport employees exposed to frequent screening. False perceptions may be addressed effectively by disseminating information regarding the insignificant exposure levels used in screening technologies and the benefits of the screening procedures in reducing threats. However, the information must be presented in a way that is understandable to all audiences. Comparing radiation doses received in passenger screening to greater, but still safe, doses used in common or familiar circumstances (e.g., a chest x-ray) is a meaningful and effective strategy, as long as the information is framed in the appropriate context. This information, which should be presented at the screening site, could be part of a public education effort.

No health risks are associated with trace-detection technologies either. However, passengers may perceive the equipment as unhealthy if it appears unclean or unsanitary. The development of passenger screening equipment and the implementation of screening procedures should include measures that minimize the risk of disease transmission.

7

Legal Issues

The Airport Security Safety Act directs the FAA to develop and implement better airport security technology. However, legal issues and challenges could arise from approval by the FAA of the use of new and more invasive passenger screening technologies under consideration. In this chapter, the panel specifically reviews the challenges that have been raised against screening technologies currently used in airports or against the introduction of similar screening and searching technologies and procedures in other contexts. The discussion focuses on the nature of these challenges, the identity of the challengers, and the judicial responses. For purposes of the review, the panel assumes that the screening devices and the personnel operating them both function effectively.

The panel identified two principal types of legal challenges in the area of passenger screening: (1) the violation of the rights of an individual, as guaranteed under the Fourth Amendment to the U.S. Constitution, and (2) injury (real or perceived) to the person or to legal interests resulting from the passenger screening process. The first type is generally referred to as an unconstitutional search. Tort[1] claims of privacy or personal injury constitute the second type of legal challenge. Each of these issues is addressed below.

In general, under the U.S. Constitution and federal and state laws, courts have upheld the right of the FAA to institute airline passenger screening procedures, even when those procedures reveal more than just the presence or absence of dangerous materials or threat objects. However, the legal problems associated with the implementation of procedures that are more intrusive than the current ones must be addressed. According to the President's Commission on Aviation Security and Terrorism, "the more security measures are imposed, the more fundamental freedoms are restricted" (PCAST, 1990). Even as this report was being written, stricter and more invasive security measures were being imposed as a result of a higher threat level (Phillips, 1995).

The material in this chapter briefly outlines and indicates the types of legal issues that have been raised. Particular legal arguments will vary according to the jurisdiction and to the factual scenario. Details of particular arguments and cases are summarized in appendix C.

UNCONSTITUTIONAL SEARCH

The Fourth Amendment to the U.S. Constitution is the most obvious context in which the legality of airport security searches is determined. Like airport security searches, the role of the Fourth Amendment is to balance privacy and law enforcement. The Fourth Amendment protects "the right of the people to be secure in their persons, houses, papers, and effects against unreasonable searches and seizures" by stipulating that any search conducted must be made on reasonable grounds. In addition to the reasonableness of the grounds, the courts commonly weigh three aspects of a search to determine whether the search is reasonable: the degree of intrusiveness of the search procedure; the magnitude and frequency of the threat; and the sufficiency of alternatives to conducting a search. Courts also consider the effectiveness of the search in reducing the threat and whether sufficient care has been taken to limit the scope of the search as much as possible, while still maintaining this effectiveness.

The analysis of a Fourth Amendment challenge involves two threshold issues: (1) whether there is a search or seizure, and (2) whether the search or seizure is done by the government. (These two concepts are discussed in more detail in appendix C.) If no search or seizure occurred, or if it was done by a private entity,[2] then it is not necessary to determine whether it was reasonable under the Fourth amendment. In such cases, the requirements of the amendment simply do not apply (see *Dow Chemical Co.*, 1986; *Lebron*, 1995).[3]

Once it has been determined that a search has been done by the government, the Fourth Amendment requires that the search must either have been supported by a warrant or that

---

[1]A tort is a wrongful act for which a civil monetary award may be assessed.

[2]Some circuits hold that "the government's involvement in promulgating the FAA guideline to combat hijacking is so pervasive as to bring any search conducted pursuant to that program within the reach of the Fourth

Amendment" (*United States v. Ross*, [9th Cir. 1994]). Other circuits hold that airline searches constitute private conduct (*United States v. Morgan*, [6th Cir. 1985]). No universal agreement has been reached as to whether airport searches are performed by the government or by private entities.

[3]A brief description of many cases cited is contained in appendix C.

it must fit into a few "specifically and well-delineated exceptions" (Katz, 1967). Of course, in the airport security context, "time limitations effectively preclude security personnel from obtaining a warrant for searching" (McGinely and Downs, 1972). Therefore, airport security searches, if they are determined to be searches in the context of the Fourth Amendment, must fit into one of three established exceptions applicable to the airport security context: the administrative search exception, the stop-and-frisk exception, and the consent exception. Other exceptions, such as exigent circumstances or a search incident to a lawful arrest based on probable cause, have been found to be applicable in the airport security context, but these will not be discussed in this report since, by their very nature, they are random and unpredictable occurrences.

Virtually all Fourth Amendment challenges to airport security screening devices and procedures have been claims made by criminal defendants seeking to exclude the evidence so obtained from criminal trials or to overturn convictions. These people were found to have had illegal items, such as drugs, on their persons or in their carry-on baggage during a security search. To prevent the use of the discovered evidence and to thwart a criminal prosecution against them, these defendants sought to suppress the evidence by alleging a violation of the Fourth Amendment; that is, that the evidence was obtained as a result of an illegal search.

Occasionally, a person who has not allegedly committed a crime, at least not in the current lawsuit, brings a civil claim for a monetary award based on Fourth Amendment protection or makes a criminal complaint against officers or agencies responsible for breaching their protection. A person or group may also sue to stop an allegedly violative process in advance (*Klarfeld*, 1992; *Hartke*, 1973; *Wagner*, 1985; *Bivens*, 1971).

Administrative Search Exception

Airport security searches fit quite naturally into the administrative search exception to the Fourth Amendment. Administrative searches are justified on the basis that they serve a societal purpose other than standard criminal law enforcement (*Vernonia School District 47J*, 1995, citing *Griffin*, 1987). After all, the Fourth Amendment cannot be construed to prevent the government from fulfilling a variety of other necessary functions, such as maintaining school discipline, preventing drunk driving, detecting illegal aliens, or even ensuring air traffic safety (*Vernonia*, 1995; *Michigan Dept. State Police*, 1990; *United States v. Martinez-Fuerte*, 1976).

The first issue that must be faced in determining whether a search scheme falls into the administrative search exception balances the privacy interests sacrificed against the societal purpose or the need for which the search scheme was undertaken. If the balance is struck on the side of the government,

it must still be determined whether the special need could have been met in a less intrusive manner. Finally, it must be determined whether the particular search was really made pursuant to the special need.

Balancing Approach

In determining whether a need justifies a general regulatory scheme of searching, the court balances the nature of the privacy interest on which the search intrudes against the nature of the government interest (*Vernonia*, 1995 at 2390, citing *Skinner*, 1989). In the case of airport passenger screening, the nature of the government interest will change according to the perceived threat level. That is, government interest in ensuring air safety is stronger during times of danger, such as when a credible threat of attack exists against a specific airport (as there was against the three New York City area airports during the writing of this report) or when the United States is involved in international conflicts (such as during the Persian Gulf War).

Even in times of relative peace, the societal interest in preventing air piracy has commonly been balanced favorably against the invasion of a search, thereby allowing the use of general passenger screening procedures (*United States v. Pulido-Baquerizo*, 1986; *United States v. Epperson*, 1972; *Camara*, 1967; *United States v. Davis*, 1973). Part of the justification for the administrative search exception to the requirement for a search warrant is the regulatory scheme for airport security searches, which requires that all persons be searched, regardless of suspiciousness of any particular individual (14 C.F.R. §107.20 [1995]). The issue considered in this report is whether that search, if performed using new technologies that are more intrusive than current technologies, will tip this balance. "Is the interest important enough to justify the particular search at hand, in light of other factors which show the search to be relatively intrusive upon a person's expectation of privacy?" (*Vernonia*, 1995 at 2394). To answer this question, we must look at the other factors in the balancing approach.

Against the special need of the government, the court must consider the passenger's expectation of privacy. This consideration involves the same analysis used in the threshold issue of whether a search has occurred, with one important difference. Deciding whether a person has a reasonable expectation of privacy for purposes of determining whether or not a search has taken place is a yes-or-no-question. Either one does or does not have a legitimate expectation of privacy in this context. On the other hand, expectation of privacy as a factor in the balancing test becomes a matter of degree. Thus, the court in *Vernonia* (1995) held that schoolchildren, because of the supervisory role schools have over them, have a decreased expectation of privacy at school. As discussed in the first section, airline passengers most probably have a legitimate expectation of privacy against being searched in an intrusive manner. Nevertheless, this expectation could decrease if passengers perceive the threat level to be high.

Another factor balanced against the special needs of the government is the nature of the privacy intrusion. Although there is a good reason for it, "the intrusion is not insubstantial. It is inconvenient and annoying, in some cases it may be embarrassing, and at times can be incriminating" (*United States v. Skipwith*, 1973). The Supreme Court is particularly sensitive to the invasiveness of the search. In supporting the drug testing of high school athletes in *Vernonia* (1995), Justice Scalia recited with some detail just how the urine samples are collected: "The student enters an empty locker room accompanied by an adult of the same sex. Each boy produces a sample of urine [while] remaining fully clothed with his back to the monitor who stands approximately 12–15 feet behind the student...no less privacy than in public restrooms" (*Vernonia*, 1995 at 2388).

For a more intrusive search, the court has not overturned Circuit Court opinions upholding strip searches in public schools (*Cornfield*, 1993; *Williams*, 1991). In these cases, the findings of the courts that the nature of the intrusion did not upset the balance in school searches is in the government's favor, but this interpretation is not universal (*State v. Mark Anthony D.*, 1993). Similarly, the extra intrusiveness of body cavity searches of prisoners did not upset the balance struck on the side of the government for prisoner searches (*Covino*, 1992). Will the extra intrusiveness of some technologies for airport security searches tip the balance in favor of privacy interests? Careful measures were taken in the situation cited in *Vernonia* (1995) to protect the privacy and dignity of the students and still meet the special needs of the government; that is, to detect and prevent drug usage among student athletes. And, in the school strip search cases, the searches were conducted only on particular suspicion of particular individuals. Unlike the drug testing upheld in *Vernonia* (1995) the school strip searches were not part of a regulatory scheme applied to an entire class of persons. Prisoners can be strip searched because the special need to do so is strong and the expectation of privacy is very low (*Covino*, 1992 at 77); airline passengers have a much higher expectation of privacy than prisoners. Given the conclusions of *Vernonia* (1995), it would seem that few general regulatory schemes could justify such invasive searches.

To justify a passenger screening technology that produces an image of passengers' bodies beneath their clothes, the screening procedures must be such that the privacy of the individual is protected to the extent possible. However, the special need of the government to ensure air travel security is certainly as strong as the need for prison security, especially at times of high threat levels. In addition, the nature of the intrusion on the privacy of airline passengers is not as invasive as the body cavity searches of prisoners. More privacy is assured in being clothed and being scanned by a machine and a possibly unseen operator than in being prodded by live guards. It seems as though the balance might strike on the side of air travel security. Nevertheless, these imaging technologies might not be acceptable if the government need for ensuring air travel security can be met through less intrusive means.

Thus, measures should be taken to minimize the appearance of nakedness, the number of people having access to and identifying the image with the traveler, the time the image endures or is preserved, the uses to be made of the data, etc., to the extent consistent with safety objectives. The next section deals with the concept of less versus more intrusive means.

Less Intrusive Alternatives

Although the interest in safety may outweigh the invasion against privacy, that invasion must still be minimized to the extent feasible because the invasion is justified only to the extent necessary to achieve the government goal of air travel safety. Therefore, it is important to ensure that the searches are made pursuant, and substantially related, to that purpose (*Vernonia*, 1995 at 2395).

The courts generally have upheld that a security search must be as "limited...as is consistent with the administrative need that justifies [it]" (*United States v. $124,570 U.S. Currency*, 1989), but practicality does not need to be sacrificed (*Vernonia*, 1995 at 2388). This concept is important for airport searches because the only alternatives to many technologies for detecting weapons and explosives are visual and tactile body searches (*United States v. Doe*, 1993; *State v. Perez*, 1987), which are obviously more invasive. Still, even intrusive searches can be conducted in a minimally intrusive manner. For example, if images of the bodies of passengers must be produced, images should be displayed no longer than necessary to ascertain the security risk. There should also be a guarantee that the image data will neither be preserved nor archived.

An example of a minimally intrusive passenger screening technique that would not be considered an invasion of privacy is scanning passengers boarding cards for traces of explosive material. Passengers receive boarding cards prior to boarding the flight, when they hand a part of the card back to an air carrier. This technique is unlikely to reveal anything about the passenger other than information about their previous handling of explosive materials.[4]

---

[4]Many legitimate reasons can be given to explain why a person would have traces of explosive or dangerous materials on their hands, including employment at an explosives manufacturing plant or in some ski areas. Thus, this search technique would not just reveal illegal activity.

Potential for Abuse

Even if more intrusive airport security-screening procedures can be justified under the administrative search exception, it still must be determined whether a particular search was so conducted pursuant to this objective. As discussed above, air travel safety is, without question, a weighty administrative objective. Yet, questions may arise about whether a particular search was appropriately conducted toward this objective.

No matter how narrowly a device or procedure is tailored to detecting safety-related concerns, other information will still be obtained in the process. The procedure may yet be acceptable if the additional information is learned inadvertently. When that information is sought specifically, however, and no concurrent safety rationale is given, then the search no longer falls under the exception. The search thus constitutes an actionable violation of constitutional rights (see discussion of *United States v. $124,570 U.S. Currency* [1989)] in appendix C). For example, security screeners may ask passengers to open carry-on bags, if the x-ray image shows a suspicious shape that may be an item dangerous to the airplane. However, it is not acceptable for screeners to inspect bags solely on the suspicion that they contain drugs or large amounts of cash. *United States v. $124,570 U.S. Currency* (1989) establishes a presumption that information unrelated to safety is sought when rewards are to be gained. On the other hand, the discovery of drugs by a security officer need not be totally inadvertent (*Horton*, 1990).

The fine point of this argument is whether information on a nonthreat object is obtained in the course of the strict search for threat objects or whether action has been taken, in the course of the search, to broaden the scope to include a search for nonthreat but illegal or suspicious objects. Current airport passenger screening techniques are open to challenges that a particular screener acted outside of the limited right to search for threat objects. Technologies that permit the identification only of items that are a threat to the safety of the airport and the aircraft would remove this subtle element of doubt in the airport screening process. These technologies would also likely be welcomed by air carriers because it means less time spent on handling claims against faulty screening procedures. Technologies that give the operator more specific information about an alarm, such as the location of a metallic object on a person's body, also would work to minimize the amount of extraneous information obtained during a search.

One way to tailor the search procedure used to a specific need is to screen specially indicated passengers. For example, invasive searches could be made only of persons who repeatedly set off metal-detector alarms. Security personnel may conduct even an intimate search of such persons until the suspicion is dispelled (*United States v. Roman-Marcon*, 1993; *State v. Baez*, 1988). As mentioned before, this invasiveness must be reduced to the extent possible.

Stop-and-Frisk Exception

A stop-and-frisk exception to the Fourth Amendment requirement for a search warrant occurs when an officer or another authority has a reasonable suspicion that another person is a threat. In the context of airport passenger screening, the *reasonable suspicion* might be that the subject fits the profile of a *typical hijacker*, or that the screener observed a bulge under the subject's jacket, which raised the suspicion that the person could be carrying a concealed weapon. Because suspicion focuses rather particularly on that individual, this may fall under the general principle of stop-and-frisk law and be called an *individual stop and frisk search*. In addition, it would seem that the law would allow a stop-and-frisk search if an individual fits a *narrow class* of suspicious persons. This we may call a *selectee class* search. Thus, anyone triggering the alarm on the metal detector would be under a reasonable suspicion and may be searched further under this exception to the Fourth Amendment. In actual application, the two kinds of stop-and-frisk searches tend to blend, and it is questionable whether even in theory they are separate. Both are based on the *Terry* case, discussed below.

Individual Stop-and-Frisk Search

In 1969, almost one Eastern Airlines flight per week was diverted by hijackers (Fenello, 1973). In response, Eastern instituted a deterrent system consisting of a metal detector and a behavioral profile. The use of this system was upheld under the standard in *Terry v. Ohio* (1968) and in *United States v. Lopez-Pages* (1971).

In *Terry* (1968) the Supreme Court ruled that a policeman, based on his own instincts and suspicions and on the need to protect himself and others, may conduct a limited search for weapons without a warrant or *probable cause* to believe there was a crime (*Terry*, 1968 at 6). Although not the level of individualized suspicion required under the rubric *probable cause*, there still had to be some reasonable grounds, and the search was limited to a frisk-type weapons pat-down. *Lopez* (1971) upheld Eastern's use of its system because of its selectivity in searching only those who fit the profile and those who had triggered the metal-detector alarm (*Lopez*, 1971 at 1080). Just as the officer in *Terry* (1968) had a particularized and objective basis for suspecting that a crime was being committed, so did the security officials of Eastern Airlines. Thus, Eastern could perform a search of a limited scope and duration for safety reasons. However, a potential for abuse exists in accepting a warrantless search in the application of the profile to an individual. To prevent abuse, the attributes in the profile must be relevant to the threat being averted.

Soon after pioneering efforts of Eastern, the mass-search technique became the order of the day. No longer was there a need to demonstrate a prior basis for suspicion and, thus, there was no need to use the stop-and frisk search, (Emergency Order of FAA, U.S. Dept. Transp. Press Release No. 103-72 [Dec. 5, 1972]; 14 C.F.R. §121.538 [1973]). The general climate of danger following the repeated hijackings of U.S. air carrier flights was determined to be reason enough for searching all airline passengers (*United States v. Epperson*, 1972). Because of its universal application to all passengers, the airport security check was naturally justified as an administrative search, and the general stop-and-frisk search exception to the Fourth Amendment for airport passenger screening was no longer needed.

Selectee Class Stop-and-Frisk Search

In contrast to the individualized stop-and-frisk search, the selectee class category of the stop-and-frisk search approach requires the identification of a small group of people singled out for additional scrutiny. In current airport security-screening procedures, passengers who set off the metal-detector alarm are automatically identified for scrutiny. As in the individualized stop-and-frisk search, the criteria used to identify these passengers must be relevant to the threat being averted.

Security personnel need only a minimal level of objective justification—something more than an inchoate and unparticularized suspicion or hunch—to conduct a selectee-type stop-and-frisk search (*United States v. Sokolow*, 1989 at 7 [quoting *Terry*, 1968]). The suspicion only needs to establish probability, not certainty, and it can be established from the totality of circumstances (*United States v. Sokolow*, 1989 [citing *United States v. Cortez*, 1981]). Thus, the requisite suspicion can be established not only by the passenger fitting the hijacker profile, but also by the passenger repeatedly triggering the metal-detector alarm (LaFave, §10.6[f]; *United States v. Lopez-Pages*, 1985).

If air carriers were able to identify potential hijackers or terrorists with some degree of accuracy, then the administrative search justification for universal screening would come into question, and airport security-screening procedures could be altered substantially. After all, there would be no need to search every passenger, if searching only a few would be enough to meet the safety goals (LaFave, at §10.6[c]). If selectivity is lacking, the stop-and-frisk justification would come into question. Because the *Terry* (1968) stop-and-frisk search is directed at persons—as opposed to the administrative search, which is directed at places—it cannot be used as a sufficient basis for searching someone simply because he or she is at the airport preparing to board a plane. This selectivity would not sufficiently distinguish between innocent passengers and individuals likely to cause security problems.

For both legal and practical reasons, under the stop-and-frisk justification the selection criteria used to identify those who could be subjected to additional screening must be such that very large percentages of the population are not identified for further investigation. Under the *Lopez* approach, only 0.28 percent of all passengers were selected, and half of them were not even stopped because they did not trigger the alarm on the metal detector. Only 6 percent of the 0.28 percent were found to be carrying weapons. These numbers are equivalent to stopping approximately 700 people at the Dallas-Fort Worth International Airport each year to identify 40 to 50 people carrying weapons. This rate of additional screening was deemed sufficient in the Lopez case in 1985 (LaFave, at §10.6[b]), and, if the selectivity criteria were highly accurate, it probably would still be sufficient today (*United States v. Sokolow*, 1989).

Some cases are more clear-cut than others. In *United States v. Dalpiaz* (1974), a passenger going through a security checkpoint was found to be carrying a pistol, a hunting knife, six bullets taped together, a walkie-talkie, a gun holster, an alarm clock, and a woman's cigarette case with a number of wires. Upon further inspection, a nonmetallic projectile-simulator explosive device was also found in his coat. Dalpiaz argued that the final search was unjustified because he had already passed the metal detector after setting the other items aside. The court rejected this argument, finding that the police had a sufficient objective basis for believing that Dalpiaz posed a safety risk to themselves and to the public.

Underlying both the administrative and the stop-and-frisk exceptions is a balancing approach. The government interest must be greater than the individual privacy lost. Because administrative searches are general regulatory schemes, the balancing is done on an aggregate level. Searching all passengers is worth it. On the other hand, the balancing for stop-and-frisk searches is done on an individual level where a particular objective basis is required for searching individuals. The balance in a stop-and-frisk case will favor privacy, unless the probability is high that the person was stopped because her or she posed a safety problem. Nevertheless, the added flexibility of the stop-and-frisk approach allows the air carrier to increase the invasiveness of the search as suspicion of an individual increases.

Consent Exception

The Fourth Amendment protects the privacy interests of people. When passengers freely and voluntarily give their consent to a security search, they surrender those interests, and there would be no question of a violation of their Fourth Amendment rights (*Schneckloth v. Bustamonte*, 1973). By consenting to the search, individuals surrender their legitimate expectation of privacy and make the search reasonable.

Explicit voluntary consent will forestall any Fourth Amendment issue. However, if "the nature of the established screening process is such that the attendant circumstances will establish nothing more than acquiescence to apparent lawful authority," some authorities have ruled that there is not real consent, (LaFave, at §10.6[g], citing *United States v. Ruiz-Estrella*, 1973). It can hardly be considered voluntary consent, some authorities argue, when a passenger's alternative to submission is forgoing his or her flight (*United States v. Albarado*, 1974).

Signs announcing air carrier search policies are posted at all security checkpoints (14 C.F.R. §108.17[e], 1995). When passengers proceed to the gate, have they implicitly consented to a search? Perhaps. (*United States v. Davis*, 1973 at 912; contra LaFave, at §10.6[g]). But a passenger wishing to board an airplane has no choice but to agree to the search. In 1991 the Supreme Court ruled that having a confined range of choices does not necessarily render consent involuntary when the individual is responsible for confining those choices (*Florida v. Bostick*, 1991). In other words, when individuals place themselves in a situation where they are likely to be searched, they could be deemed to have consented to the search.

Airline passengers would not feel free to decline a request to submit to a search because declining the search means declining the right to fly. Yet passengers approach the security officers and place themselves in a situation in which they know they will be searched (Cf. *Vernonia*, 1987 at 2392). Although passengers may not feel free to decline the search request when they show up at the gate, they are not coerced by the government to fly in the first place. It could be argued that the airport security officers are simply part of the background into which passengers voluntarily inject themselves. And yet making the price of refusal to be searched very high (forgo the flight) is tantamount to coercion. But *Florida v. Bostick* (1991) may mean that aviation security personnel "are free to rely on coercive tactics to obtain consent [e.g., by preventing boarding] to search as long as the citizen himself contributed in some way, even innocently, to the coerciveness of the encounter [by deciding to fly]" (Heureman, 1994). However, it is too early to tell what all this conflict of arguments and authority may mean. Nevertheless, there is at least an *argument* of consent here.

Two questions regarding the consent exception remain unanswered: (1) the point at which passengers give consent, and (2) to what, precisely, passengers are consenting. (We assume from here on that there is some kind of voluntary consent implicit in the airport circumstance and examine the authority that so holds to answer these two questions.)

The first question is relatively easy to answer. Passengers are deemed to have given consent when they place their bags on the conveyer belt for luggage screening (*United States v. Pulido-Baquerizo*, 1986; *People v. Heimel*, 1991). After this point, passengers are no longer free to leave. Thus, if passengers set off the alarm on the metal detector, they must also submit to a limited manual search to determine the cause of the alarm (*People v. Heimel*, 1991; but see *United States v. Vigil*, cert. denied, 1993). If passengers were allowed to withdraw after setting off the security system, then the deterrent effect of the security system would be undermined. "There is no guarantee that...[they] might not return and be more successful. Of greater importance, the very fact that a safe exit is available...would, by diminishing the risk, encourage attempts" (*United States v. Skipwith*, 1973 [Aldrich, J., dissenting]).

The second question is more difficult to answer. Implicit consent derives much of its justification from the fact that it is a "privacy invasion [that] free society is willing to tolerate as long as the scope of the search is limited to discover[ing] weapons or explosives...and is limited in a manner which produces negligible social stigma" (*United States v. Pulido-Baquerizo*, 1986 at 901). As the search becomes more intrusive, it becomes more difficult to suppose that one would have consented to it (*United States v. Blake*, 1989), but we are not talking *real* consent here. The scope of consent is only what the reasonable person would expect (*Florida v. Jimeno*, 1991), but again, we are talking policy rather than consent. And, as discussed in the section on the expectation of privacy, what persons expect can be shaped by either edict or systematic practice.

Other Exceptions to Fourth Amendment Requirements

In addition to the exceptions cited above for conducting a search without a warrant, officials may conduct warrantless searches under a few other circumstances. For example, at a national border, a U.S. Customs official is allowed to "stop, search, and examine any person upon whom an officer suspects there is contraband" (19 U.S.C. §482, 1994; *United States v. Ramsey*, 1977). Another such scenario involves exigent circumstances or an emergency. Searches under exigent circumstances are conducted to prevent physical harm to officers or other persons (*United States v. Sarkissian*, 1988; Ayres, 1994). Thus, when the government need is greater or more urgent, a search can be justified, and the invasiveness of a search can be increased. We have also put to one side the exception allowing a search pursuant to a lawful arrest, as stated above.

TORT CLAIMS

The employment of new airport security technologies, especially those that produce images of passengers' bodies beneath their clothes, might provoke two types of tort claim: claims for personal injuries caused by the operation of the device, and claims for violations of personal privacy. Because torts are governed by state law, the variety of claims in particular factual scenarios and in particular jurisdictions may vary widely. Therefore, a few general issues are discussed below. Anyone facing a specific claim, of course, must get professional legal help addressed specifically to the particular facts, which may make an enormous difference.

A threshold issue in both types of tort claim is whether the FAA has immunity under the Federal Tort Claims Act (28 U.S.C. §2680) and whether this immunity extends to the air carrier or the security company operating the screening equipment or to the manufacturer of the equipment. The FAA is probably immune from any tort suit, if it is acting within its discretionary function (28 U.S.C. §2680[a]). What is discretionary is subject to a long line of cases, but negligence on an operational level or in carrying out something in a particular case is probably not a discretionary function. Most of what is considered here, however, probably would be a discretionary function, i.e., adopting certain policies and guidelines. But even then, it is not possible to be definitive. Air carriers and manufacturers have also been found to be not liable in certain instances (but not all) where the immunity conferred on the Federal Aviation Administration may be extended to private actors acting pursuant to government directives (28 U.S.C. §1671; *Carley v. Wheeled Coach*, 1993). For reasons unrelated to immunity, security companies on some occasions (but not all) have been found not to be liable for damages caused by the security-screening process because security companies have no control over the configuration of the device; the companies merely operate it for the air carrier, without the authority to change anything on or about the device (*Klopp v. Wackenhut Corporation*, 1992).

The above discussion of situations of non-liability refers only to the *policy* of airport security screening. Under other circumstances, manufacturers or operators may be found liable for injury due to the operation, maintenance, inspection, etc., of the security equipment. If an air carrier properly deploys and operates a metal detector that satisfies the requirements set forth by the FAA for such devices, then the air carrier is probably not liable for damage or invasion resulting from a potential claimant's passage through it if the equipment is working properly. Liability for a person carrying a threat object the metal detector *was not* designed to detect is probably similar, unless the claimant makes an argument that some other measures should have been taken. However, if the air carrier operated the equipment in a manner that allowed the passage of a person carrying a threat object that the metal detector was designed to detect, then the air carrier could be held liable for damages resulting from its failure to prevent that person from entering the sterile or *safe* area of the airport.

Product Liability

Manufacturers and operators of a wide variety of products have been found liable for injuries or perceived injuries resulting from the use of their products. The panel does not expect liability issues to be any different for manufacturers and operators of airport security-screening equipment. At the very least these companies will be required to maintain the standards maintained by other producers in the United States.

One issue that anyone suing the manufacturer or operator of security-screening equipment will have to prove is that the injury resulted from the use of the equipment. This may be difficult to do in the case of airport security-screening equipment because the exposure to, or contact with, the equipment is usually limited to a short time in a well-supervised area. However, manufacturers and operators of security-screening equipment must be aware of potential injuries resulting from their use.

An example of a technology that individuals may perceive as harmful is x-ray backscatter imaging, which exposes passengers to less than 0.003 millirem of radiation per scan (IRT Corp., n.d.). This radiation dose is 100 times less than the amount of radiation absorbed from being in Miami for one day or from watching television for one hour; it is over 300 times less than the amount absorbed during a two-hour flight (IRT Corp., n.d.). Therefore, tracing the cause of any injury to the airport security scan is difficult, as has been proven in previous cases involving common sources of radiation (*San Diego Gas & Electric Co. v. Superior Court*, 1995; *Reynard v. NEC Corporation*, 1995).

Moreover, even if causation could be proved, the FAA has extensive regulations regarding radiation emissions of x-ray devices (14 C.F.R. §108.17 [1995]). That a device satisfies these regulations will serve as strong evidence, but not proof, that the device is not defective (Restatement [Second] of Torts § 288 C, 1977). However, merely satisfying the FAA regulations regarding radiation dose limits does not necessarily mean that a device cannot cause damage to people or to their property. Thus, manufacturers and operators cannot rely on these regulations to shield them from lawsuits involving radiation exposure.

Privacy

As discussed in an earlier section of this chapter, federal constitutional rights, such as the Fourth Amendment, are rights that individuals have to protect themselves against government actions. Tort rights, on the other hand, are rights that individuals have against a wide variety of entities, such as private persons and business entities, in addition to the government. Thus, while the Fourth Amendment protects an individual's privacy from unjustified government intrusion, privacy torts protect an individual's privacy from other individuals, including the government. In many states, law similar to the following exists: "One who intentionally intrudes, physically or otherwise, upon the solitude or seclusion of another or his private affairs or concerns, is subject to liability to the other for invasion of his privacy, if the intrusion would be highly offensive to a reasonable person" (Rest. 2d Torts §652B, 1977; *Carter v. Innisfree Hotel*, 1995; *Harkey v. Abate*, 1984).

These cases might seem irrelevant to airport security screening performed in an airline terminal. Nevertheless, "even in a public place...there may be some matters about the plaintiff, such as his underwear or lack of it, that are not exhibited to the public gaze, and there may still be intrusion of privacy when there is intrusion upon these matters" (Rest. 2d Torts §652B, 1977). On the other hand, the ordinary inconveniences and annoyances facing modern society are not actionable. As discussed in the first section, what is considered an *ordinary* inconvenience is a highly individual perception that changes with experience and the perceived level of threat.

Passenger screening technologies that reveal personal details may allow individuals to sue for damages, if they believe the information was used "improperly," or the search conducted without sufficient justification or in an excessive manner or scope. Operators of this type of equipment need to be aware of the necessity to protect individual privacy during security screening to minimize this type of action.

ROLE OF THE FAA

In passenger screening, the role of the FAA is significantly different from the role of the airport operators, the air carriers, or the contracting companies performing passenger screening for the air carriers. The FAA directs air carriers to perform a certain function. The FAA does not mandate the use of a particular equipment for performing that function. However, the FAA tests each piece of passenger screening equipment to certify that it meets the established performance criteria after it is installed in an airport. The FAA also tests metal-detector portals to assure their proper operation after they have been moved to a new location in the airport. (To assist air carriers in selecting screening equipment that will satisfy FAA requirements, the FAA maintains a list of vendors who sell such equipment. Air carriers, however, are not required to choose from this list, as long as the equipment, as installed in the airport, meets the FAA performance criteria.)

Current passenger screening technologies appear to have been effective in preventing dangerous items from being carried onto airplanes. If the FAA mandates performance criteria that compel air carriers to purchase new passenger screening equipment based on new technology, then air carriers will require the FAA to demonstrate that a rational basis exists for the new criteria and that the new criteria are not arbitrary. This requirement will most likely lead to the need for new standards, in accordance with the Administrative Procedures Act, as was required for the certification of explosives detection systems.

SOME POSSIBLE LEGAL CONCERNS ASSOCIATED WITH SPECIFIC SCREENING TECHNOLOGIES

Imaging Technologies

Imaging technologies, by their very nature, reveal much more about a person than other current passenger screening technologies. This is especially so because imaging technologies require operators to view the image. The greater possibility of discovering illegal, but nonthreat, items on a person opens the door for future illegal search and seizure accusations similar to those now encountered primarily in the area of baggage inspection. Guidelines calling for operators to focus only on objects that may be a threat to the airplane may be even more difficult to follow when operators are confronted by the image of an individual carrying a broad array of articles on their person. Fourth Amendment challenges based on illegal search or on an improperly carried out search must be expected when these technologies are implemented in airports.

Concerns have been raised not only over the image revealing everything a person is carrying, but also over health risks from exposure to the radiation used to create these images. Air carriers and their contracting screening companies must be prepared to demonstrate that their equipment operates within the radiation dose range specified by the manufacturer and that these levels are safe for all people.

Some of the imaging technologies now being investigated have the capability either to store the image data for future reconstruction or to print the image and create a permanent copy. These features are appropriate for a system employed to screen people entering a correctional facility. The unauthorized possession of weapons in a correctional facility is a federal offense, and the image data may be used as evidence in the prosecution of this crime. However, this ability to store and reproduce images may create the urge to archive data on people entering airports and to store the data at least until all flights have arrived safely at their destinations. The archiving of personal data on innocent persons probably would open the air carrier and its security contracting company to legal action, based on invasion of privacy. Data obtained using these imaging technologies will be highly sensitive, and issues involving their handling and disposal must be resolved before these technologies are implemented to screen people in airports.

Some people may also be concerned about the external medical devices revealed in the images. Operators could even focus on these devices because they could be used to conceal a threat object. With current passenger screening techniques, individuals receive little attention until they set off the metal-detection portal alarm. When that happens, individuals are usually asked to empty their pockets. Most objects that set off the metal detector are common, everyday items such as keys or shoes. While most people choose not to display the contents of their pockets casually, there normally is little objection to being asked to take out keys, money, or other objects that people carry with them. The resolution of an unidentifiable object in the image, which may or may not be a medical device, will be more difficult and probably more personal. Concerns over invasion of privacy are substantially stronger when personal medical conditions are involved.

Trace-Detection Technologies

Trace-detection technologies, to the extent that they can be made specific to detection of threat materials, are not expected to raise more legal problems than current passenger screening technologies. As in the case of imaging technologies, trace-detection technologies may reveal the presence of certain medicines because many of them are closely related chemically to explosive materials. Again, questions involving invasion of privacy will be raised as innocent materials are identified.

Trace-detection technologies capable of identifying chemical signatures may also be used to identify the chemical signatures of illegal drugs. The use of this capability in the airport would constitute an illegal search because airport searches are authorized only to identify objects or materials that are a threat to the safety of the airplane. Air carriers and their contract security companies must be careful to ensure that their equipment is not designed or modified to detect materials that are not considered threat items in the context of airport and air travel security. People may also perceive a health or other threat (e.g., germs) from trace-detection technologies that contact the person, especially if many are contacted without cleansing between persons. Tort lawsuits based on uncleanliness are possible.

Nonimaging Electromagnetic Technologies

Assuming improvements in current passenger screening devices do not change the passenger-system interface appreciably, there should be no reason to expect major differences between the current and future legal issues associated with nonimaging electromagnetic technologies. Indeed, if the technology improved so that only threat objects would be identified, there would be less basis to support a claim of an illegal search, on the theory that individuals cannot legitimately have expectation of privacy for illegal items. Technologies designed to more specifically locate and identify threat objects, other than those that will trigger alarms in present-day systems, reduces some of the legal concerns over this type of passenger screening.

Nonimaging dielectric portals based on microwave irradiation are likely to raise health concerns similar to those raised over the imaging technologies, but without the concerns about image data storage and projection.

SUMMARY

Legal questions surrounding the implementation of new passenger screening technologies fall into two categories: (1) potential claims of violations against an individual's right to protection from unreasonable search as specified under the Fourth Amendment to the U.S. Constitution and (2) potential claims of injury to physical or other interests due to the screening process.[5]

In general, courts have found that current screening technologies constitute a reasonable search under the administrative search exception to the Fourth Amendment, even if the search reveals personal information other than the presence or absence of dangerous materials. New technologies are likely to be considered in the same light, taking into account the degree of intrusiveness of the search procedure, the magnitude and frequency of the threat, and the sufficiency of alternatives to the search or screening procedure. The courts also will consider the effectiveness of the search in reducing the threat and whether sufficient care has been taken to conduct the search as narrowly as possible, while maintaining effectiveness. Technologies that specifically identify only threat objects are likely to face the fewest legal obstacles. New technologies used as a secondary screening technique (i.e., used only for screening specially profiled passengers or those who set off the portal metal-detector alarm) probably will fall under the stop-and-frisk exception to the warrant requirements of the Fourth Amendment to the U.S. Constitution.

Tort claims are difficult to make in the context of passenger screening for several reasons. First, the FAA and the air carriers who operate security equipment for screening mandated by the FAA frequently have a claim of immunity if they are acting under the discretionary function of the FAA. Second, it is probably difficult to prove that the passenger screening device or process caused the injury. However, manufacturers and operators of security-screening equipment cannot assume they have impunity. As with any product used by the general public, manufacturers and operators must be aware of potential injuries resulting from the use of their products.

Many of the legal issues discussed in this chapter are less of a concern to the FAA than to air carriers operating the screening checkpoints or hiring contractors to operate them. In the case of current screening technologies, the legality of

---

[5]Although not discussed, in the latter category there may also be tort claims for assault and battery, false imprisonment, trespass to chattel, negligence, *fear* of injury (as opposed to actual injury), etc. But assuming the procedures are properly justified, manufactured, deployed, and operated, viable defenses will probably present themselves.

the search itself usually has been upheld, but questions frequently have been raised regarding the screening procedure used in individual cases. Air carriers and contracting companies would benefit from technologies that issue fewer false alarms and more specific alarms to allow personnel to resolve alarms without gaining irrelevant information. New performance criteria, which require the use of new technologies, may be of concern to the FAA if the only way air carriers can satisfy the new criteria would be to violate an individual's rights under the Fourth Amendment. In that case, the FAA may be enjoined from mandating such performance criteria. The FAA must also ensure that new performance criteria are reasonable and consistent with the statutory authority of the FAA to impose such measures.

8

Public Acceptance

The public acceptance issues associated with new passenger screening technologies focus on the extent to which people are willing to tolerate the screening procedures. While a screening technology and its operator may function properly, the ultimate success of the procedure requires its acceptance by the people being screened. The term *people* does not refer to a homogeneous body but to a group that includes airline passengers, friends and relatives of passengers, flight crews, and airport and air carrier employees. Some people are exposed to screening infrequently, while others are screened more often. Thus, these two groups may react quite differently to the implementation of a new screening technology.

As discussed in the introductory chapter, the concerns of people exposed to screening technologies can be expected to fall under four broad categories: health (exemplified by concerns about exposure to radiation), convenience, privacy (encompassing both possessions and the person's body)[1] and comfort. Public acceptance of the passenger screening technologies described in chapter 3 will also depend on the extent to which they are viewed as successful in providing security and on the degree to which that security is seen as necessary.

PUBLIC CONCERNS ABOUT HEALTH EFFECTS

The health issues associated with the technologies under consideration are discussed in chapter 6. Health concerns over active imaging technologies and over dielectric portals result more from negative perceptions of risk than from actual health threats. Although the technologies do not pose a health problem, people may believe that they do. This perception may be strong especially among aircrews and airport employees exposed to frequent screening as part of their employment. Such perceptions of risk may be addressed effectively by providing information regarding the insignificant exposure levels involved in the technologies. However, the information must be presented in a way that is understandable to a wide variety of audiences. Comparing radiation doses used in passenger screening to greater, but still safe, doses used in common or familiar procedures usually is a meaningful and

effective approach. Such information should be presented at the screening site, perhaps as part of a public education effort.

Health concerns over trace-detection technologies center on potential disease transmission through contacts either between individuals or between people being screened and the equipment. Although the health hazards appear insignificant, the screening equipment should be designed to allow frequent cleaning to minimize passenger-to-passenger disease transmission and the public perception of an unhealthy environment. Health concerns related to nonimaging electromagnetic portals have more to do with risk perception than with actual health threats. Again, in the context of such technologies, public perceptions can, and should, be addressed through public information and education.

PUBLIC CONCERNS ABOUT PRIVACY

Privacy is likely to be the most significant public acceptance issue associated with imaging technologies. Displaying an image of the body on a monitor will obviously be of concern to a significant percentage of people passing through screening checkpoints. This concern may be greater among flight crews and airport employees who are screened more frequently and who may be known to or familiar with the operators. It is important to address this concern before imaging technologies can gain acceptance. Steps to alleviate concerns may include:

- masking portions of the displayed image or distorting the image to make it appear less "human"
- using operators of the same sex as the subject to view the images
- displaying the images out of the view of everyone except the screening personnel
- providing guarantees that the images will not be preserved beyond the brief screening procedure, except when questionable objects are detected
- offering alternative screening procedures for those who object to imaging

Privacy concerns associated with trace-detection technologies appear to fall into two categories. The first category involves concerns over information revealed in the screening

---

[1]As a general rule, privacy is a more significant issue for women than for men.

process that subjects may wish to keep private, such as the presence of a medical device or the use of nitroglycerin or other medications. To address these concerns over privacy, trace-detection technologies should be adapted, as specifically as possible, to the threat being investigated.

The second category involves the aversion of some people to being touched, either with an inanimate object, such as a bar or a frond, or by a person wielding a hand-wand device. This concern is more difficult to address because the desire to maintain distance from strangers is a deeply ingrained response that is often influenced by basic cultural and religious beliefs. The *optimum* distance that people preserve between themselves and others varies greatly from person to person and from culture to culture, and it is unlikely to be swayed by public information campaigns. For procedures requiring contact between the screening personnel and the person being screened, it is important for the screener to maintain a professional attitude. Same-sex screening would probably make the procedure more acceptable to some people. For technologies requiring passengers to touch a piece of equipment, passenger acceptance may be enhanced by allowing subjects to control the area to be touched (e.g., letting them push doors open with their hands), instead of having them walk through a portal lined with fronds that brush against the entire body. The former approach, however, will restrict sample collection significantly and could result in less effective screening.

Because nonimaging metal-detection portals are already being used in airports, the panel does not expect concerns over privacy, beyond those that may exist today, to emerge from the use of improved versions of this technology. The nonimaging dielectric portals, similarly, would raise few concerns about privacy. Indeed, if the technology could be made more specific to detecting threat objects, then passengers would be less concerned about invasions to their privacy. For example, people would no longer be forced to empty their pockets at the security checkpoint.

PUBLIC CONCERNS ABOUT CONVENIENCE

As noted earlier in the report, convenience is largely a matter of time. Given that people in airports are often in a hurry and concerned with time, screening technologies that impose delays will have problems with public acceptance. Carry-on baggage screening technologies currently impose a delay of approximately six seconds, in addition to any time spent waiting in line to place carry-on bags onto conveyor belts. Technologies able to process people in six seconds or less are not likely to be a problem because passengers are already accustomed to such time delays. Nonimaging electromagnetic and microwave technologies are consistent with this time goal. Current uses of the imaging technologies under consideration (e.g., for screening persons entering

correctional facilities) do not impose time constraints. However, it is not known whether these technologies can be used to screen a passenger in approximately six seconds, including time for creating and interpreting the image. Trace-detection technologies, especially the sampling techniques under consideration are much less mature in the area of passenger screening, and the ability of these technologies to meet the *six-second* goal is unknown.

PUBLIC CONCERNS ABOUT COMFORT

Issues related to comfort will generally arise for technologies that require people to be in close contact with either the equipment or with other people; people usually do not like to be touched. For example, implementing a technology that requires a passenger to stand in an enclosed space for screening is likely to cause comfort concerns. Technologies that involve touching a person with an object, such as walking through a portal lined with fronds that brush against the body, may also make people uncomfortable. However, giving people more control over the area to be touched, such as allowing them to push a door open with their hands, may cause less apprehension.

Imaging technologies or nonimaging electromagnetic and microwave technologies implemented in an enclosed area might raise concerns over passenger comfort, but trace-detection technologies are more likely to cause such concerns because they require either physical contact or confined airflow. Technologies that incorporate physical contact between the person being screened and the equipment or the human operator will probably raise more concern over comfort than those that do not. Current implementation possibilities for trace-detection technologies include contact portals and hand-wand devices. Portals necessitate close contact between the person being screened and the screening equipment; hand-wand devices require close contact between the person being screened and the screening operator. As with the privacy issues, the comfort issues associated with contact trace technologies may prove to be a significant implementation hurdle because the desire to keep an *optimum* distance from other people and objects is deeply ingrained. The optimum distance depends on a wide variety of factors, including culture, gender, and status and is unlikely to be altered by a public education campaign.

Technologies that collect samples by using airflow rather than through physical contact will create less apprehension, but they may not be as effective as technologies that require contact. Technologies that can take advantage of a secondary source of particulates (e.g., by analyzing boarding passes or the handles of carry-on bags) would also be more acceptable to the average passenger than technologies that require physical contact.

ASSESSING PUBLIC ACCEPTANCE

The analysis of public acceptance issues is based on the work of the panel, as outlined in chapter 2, the methodology section. Further efforts to assess public acceptance of a particular technology and to incorporate this information into the screening system using that technology will be necessary to ensure effective performance.

Conducting the assessment presents a relatively complex and difficult problem. The degree to which people will accept the inconvenience, discomfort, delays, embarrassment, real or perceived health risks, and the real or perceived invasions of their privacy associated with passenger screening depends on the interaction of several variables. The variables that affect public acceptance of specific screening systems and procedures include the following:

- the nature, extent, and likelihood of the actual threat and the associated risks
- the degree of understanding and the perception of the actual threat and the associated risks
- personal beliefs, habits, and cultural mores
- the physical, mental, and emotional state of an individual
- the extent and degree of public understanding of the screening objectives, technology, and procedures
- public perception of the effectiveness of the screening system
- public understanding and perception of the health risks associated with the screening system
- the nature and frequency of air travel

One way to assess public acceptance of alternative screening systems and procedures is to conduct a survey of the population most likely to be affected by passenger screening. However, obtaining useful, definitive results from such a survey involves significant difficulties because of the potential extent of sampling and measurement error. Sampling error, or the extent to which the sample selected for measurement differs in significant ways from the population sampled, may be substantial due to difficulties in determining the relevant dimensions of the population and the difficulties of sampling the population, once it has been identified. Measurement error, or the extent to which error is introduced by the measurement process itself, is likely to be great due to the difficulties people have in responding to abstract, future (as opposed to concrete, here-and-now) circumstances.

We can identify important issues of public acceptance by identifying similar or analogous circumstances of the past and studying available information on public reaction to, and acceptance of, these circumstances. For example, we can gain insight from the public reaction to, and acceptance of, metal detectors and baggage screeners when they were first introduced. The more recent introduction of imaging screening systems that see through clothing and display images of the bodies of individuals entering correctional institutions can serve as the basis for gaining insight on issues associated with public reaction to, and acceptance of, this passenger-system interface.

Definitive estimates of public acceptance, however, must await the experimental field evaluation of prototype systems. Consequently, it will be important, as part of these field experiments, to include measures of public reaction and acceptance using measurement instruments that have been designed and tested by professionals with expertise in psychometrics.

RESULTS OF THE WORKSHOP ON NEW TECHNOLOGIES FOR PASSENGER SCREENING

The specific concerns identified during the workshop described in chapter 2 are summarized in tables 8-1 and 8-2. In preparing the tables, the possible passenger-system interfaces were first specified for each of the three principal screening technologies currently under consideration—imaging, trace, and nonimaging electromagnetic. Then, the health, privacy, comfort, and convenience concerns identified in the workshop were listed for each interface. Some of the categories of concern are not applicable to a particular technology; for example, the effects of radiation on the body would not be a concern under any of the trace-detection technologies.

The people invited to participate in the workshop represented a variety of organizations with an interest in passenger screening technologies, either because they have responsibilities in the implementation of the screening systems (e.g., air carriers and airports) or because they represent people who interact with these technologies on a regular basis (e.g., flight attendants). The workshop participants were all familiar with the operations of a passenger screening checkpoint and with various technologies considered in the past for use in passenger or baggage screening. Therefore, the reactions of these participants to the new technologies are not broadly representative of the reactions of the general public, who are not likely to be as *technically literate* or as highly motivated to find better technical solutions to the problem of ensuring airport security. As new technologies move closer to the stage where answers to specific implementation issues will be needed, the concerns expressed in the workshop can be used as guidelines to aid the FAA in identifying appropriate groups and appropriate questions to obtain information about a particular technology.

Health Effects of Radiant Energy from Imaging Technologies

A principal concern expressed early in the workshop was the potential effects of radiant energy from imaging technologies on the body, particularly in cases of pregnant women.

TABLE 8-1 Principal Concerns Associated with Health and Privacy, as Identified at the Workshop on New Technologies for Passenger Screening

| | | Potential concerns | | | |
| | | Health | | | Privacy | |
Screening technology	Passenger-System Interface	Harmful effects of radiant energy on the body	Risk of communicable disease transmission	Displeasure at being touched by sampling devices that appear unclean	Reluctance to permit body body image to be displayed to a human inspector	Possible unlawful search and seizure, if other than threat objects are detected and acted upon
Imaging	A human inspector views a display of an image of the passenger's body under layers of clothing to detect firearms or explosives	X	—	—	X	X
Trace	A human inspector moves a hand-held wand over the clothed body of the passenger, touching the passenger, to detect traces of explosives	—	X	—	—	X
Trace	Passengers pass through a portal that touches part of their bodies to detect traces of explosives	—	X	X	—	X
Trace	Passengers pass through a portal that blows air past their bodies to detect traces or vapors of explosives	—	—	—	—	X
Electromagnetic	Passengers pass through a portal that employs electromagnetic energy to detect metal objects	—	—	—	—	X
Electromagnetic	A human inspector moves a hand-held wand over the clothed body of the passenger without touching the passenger, to detect metal objects	—	—	—	—	X

Legend: — This concern is not applicable to the specific technology under consideration.

TABLE 8-2 Principal Concerns Associated with Comfort and Convenience, as Identified at the Workshop on New Technologies for Passenger Screening

		Potential Concerns			
		Comfort		Convenience	
Screening technology	Passenger-system interface	Discomfort from being enclosed in a small space	Displeasure and discomfort from the effects of blasts of air used to obtain samples	Delays imposed by inspection and system-processing time technology	Delays encountered during high-traffic or high-detection periods
Imaging	A human inspector views a display of an image of the passenger's body under layers of clothing to detect firearms or explosives	—	—	X	—
Trace	A human inspector moves a hand-held wand over the clothed body of the passenger, touching the passenger, to detect traces of explosives	—	—	X	—
Trace	Passengers pass through a portal that touches part of their bodies to detect traces of explosives	—	—	X	—
Trace	Passengers pass through a portal that blows air past their bodies to detect traces of explosives	X	X	X	—
Electromagnetic	Passengers pass through a portal that employs electromagnetic energy to detect metal objects	—	—	—	X
Electromagnetic	A human inspector moves a hand-held wand over the clothed body of the passenger, without touching the passenger, to detect metal objects	—	—	—	X

Legend: — This concern is not applicable to the specific technology under consideration.

Information presented on the small amounts of radiation involved in the application of imaging technologies, relative to amounts from other sources, appeared to allay these concerns. Specific information on comparative radiation dose levels associated with specific concerns, such as the effects on pregnant women and on pacemaker devices, will be required before these techniques can be implemented.

Displaying Images of the Bodies of Subjects

In the opinion of the workshop participants, imaging technology that requires a human inspector to view the image of a passenger's body is likely to face considerable opposition from passengers, unless steps are taken to assure anonymity and unless the level of threat is perceived to be relatively high. During the workshop, several solutions were offered to make such screening more acceptable:

- Ensure that the inspector is of the same sex as the passenger being screened.
- Ensure that the inspector is situated so the passengers and inspectors cannot see each other directly.
- Mask or eliminate sensitive areas of the passenger's body from the display, if this can be done without reducing the effectiveness of the screening.
- Represent body parts on the display in a way that reduces recognizability without reducing the effectiveness of the screening.
- Display the image only if a human inspector is needed to resolve an automatic detection alarm.

Most workshop participants said they would accept the invasion of privacy that these imaging technologies would require if the level of threat were high. Quantifying the threat level at which these technologies would be acceptable for general screening is a difficult task. This is an area that the FAA will need to explore if these technologies prove to meet other requirements for successful implementation.

Possible Unlawful Search and Seizure

A concern expressed during the workshop was that all passenger screening was in violation of the Fourth Amendment to the Constitution of the United States. As noted in chapter 7, the courts have not reached a clear consensus on the legality of these searches. However, in general, the courts have weighed the balance between the individual's right not to be searched without particularized probable cause against the public's right to be protected from air piracy and have decided in favor of the air carriers and the FAA. There was further concern that the searches could go beyond the specific stated objective of passenger screening, that is, the detection

of firearms, explosives, or other items of danger to the aircraft, crew, and passengers. In the extreme case of providing only for aircraft safety, a law enforcement officer called by security personnel to investigate a questionable item, which is later determined to be illegal drugs and not a threat to the aircraft, should ignore the presence of the drugs because they were not the object of the screening. The courts have not supported disregarding evidence of criminal behavior once a person has been stopped in an airport security checkpoint for the possible possession of a threat object. There are many sides to this debate, and new screening technologies are not likely to allay concerns about government surveillance of the innocent act of boarding an airplane.

Time Required for Passenger Screening

It was the consensus of workshop participants that the sensitivity and vulnerability of the entire air transportation system to procedures that will significantly hinder passenger progress through the system was more important than other concerns about passenger acceptance. According to air carrier, airport, and security services representatives, the complexities and interdependencies of the system are now of sufficient magnitude that a delay lasting a few seconds in the screening of an individual passenger can lead to a significant reduction in system efficiency and increases in system costs.

One side effect of the need to maintain acceptable levels of passenger throughput is the potential for less effective screening during times of high passenger volume. According to one workshop attendee, long lines at current checkpoints that use metal-detection portals and carry-on baggage screening systems bring pressure from management personnel to move people through more quickly, thus making it more difficult for the screening system to function effectively.

SOME POSSIBLE PUBLIC ACCEPTANCE CONCERNS ASSOCIATED WITH SPECIFIC SCREENING TECHNOLOGIES

Imaging Technologies

Active imaging technologies involve the use of electromagnetic radiation, such as x–rays, to produce images of individuals and objects that may be concealed under clothing. The use of any type of electromagnetic radiation, regardless of the dose applied, will raise concerns about possible biological damage due to radiation. As discussed earlier, the radiation doses used for any of the screening technologies being investigated are smaller than the amount of radiation received from many common and commonly accepted sources. This information needs to be communicated to passengers and security-screening checkpoint operators to enable them to put the risks of the screening procedure in perspective. However, this public education effort will need to consider that people distinguish between radiation received voluntarily (in medical circumstances or transcontinental flights) and radiation received involuntarily (from living in areas built over uranium mill tailings or receiving fallout from nuclear weapons tests). Passive imaging technologies are not likely to generate any health concerns because they scan for radiation naturally emitted by the human body.

In addition to concerns over the biological effects of radiation, people will be concerned with privacy issues related to the exposure of the images of their bodies. People will want to know who will see the images and how the data from the images will be handled. Using operators of the same sex to view the image and situating the operator in a remote location (far from the individual being screened) will increase public acceptance. However, these measures to accommodate the public will create implementation problems. Same-sex viewing will require more operators than currently employed. In addition, moving the operator to a remote location will require more space and additional personnel because a separate operator also must be stationed at the checkpoint to help resolve alarms and to direct passengers through the system.

Since imaging technologies use data to create an electronic image of a person, that data could be manipulated to make the image appear less *human*. This could be done perhaps by rearranging the body parts on the screen or by distorting the image to make the body appear unnaturally tall and thin. This type of distortion, achieved by distancing the image from the actual person, might make these technologies more acceptable to people who object to having images of their bodies displayed. People trained to detect threat objects on this type of distorted image may be effective screeners. Research into how much image distortion is feasible, without compromising screening effectiveness, may yield answers to help improve public acceptance of imaging technologies. Assurances must also be given that the data used to create the images will not be archived in any way and will be erased as soon as the person has been cleared to enter the secure part of the airport.

Another possible concern associated with imaging technologies is the revelation of external medical devices worn by some people. These devices will appear on the images and may even call the attention of an operator because they could be used to conceal a threat object. For these people, it may be essential to have a remotely located screener and to have the image displayed as privately as possible.

Imaging technologies may be slower than current screening techniques, especially if multiple views are required. Increasing the time needed to screen each passenger will result in added passenger inconvenience as long lines and longer waiting times become common in airports during peak periods. Air carriers and airport operators will resist the implementation of any technology requiring them to add space for passengers to stand in line at screening checkpoints or to add more checkpoints to keep waiting time to a minimum. Passenger waiting time and delay will be minimized if these technologies can be implemented in such a way that the screener immediately has a 360° view of the person being screened. However, passengers are likely to object if obtaining the view means screening the subject in an enclosed space.

Trace-Detection Technologies

The use of trace-detection technologies in passenger screening settings may involve person-to-person contact or direct contact between the detection equipment (e.g., trace-chemical sensor) and the individual. As discussed earlier, this contact can lead to concerns over the possible transmission of disease as a result of the contact. Passenger acceptance will be affected by the appearance and cleanliness of the equipment. Few privacy concerns have been associated with trace-detection technologies. However, these technologies may reveal the use of some medications, which may cause embarrassment to the passenger. Alarm-resolution techniques that allow for privacy may help to alleviate this concern.

If the trace-detection technologies for passenger screening can be implemented using a walk-through portal, then they are not expected to be any more inconvenient than current passenger screening technologies. However, if the technology requires a closed space for air collection, passengers may resist due both to the discomfort of being in an enclosed space and to the perception of added delay.

Nonimaging Electromagnetic Technologies

As discussed in earlier chapters, improvements in current passenger screening devices are not expected to change the passenger-system interface appreciably. Technologies designed to locate and identify specific threat objects, rather than a variety of objects that trigger the alarms of present-day systems, will result in increased privacy and added convenience for the passenger.

Nonimaging microwave technologies are likely to raise concerns about using microwave radiation to detect threat objects. As with the imaging technologies, this issue is more about risk perception than actual risk, and approaches to allaying passenger concerns about the use of radiation for imaging technologies would be appropriate for the dielectric portals.

SUMMARY

Four categories of issues seem most relevant to public acceptance of passenger screening technologies: health, privacy, convenience, and comfort. Health concerns are more of a risk perception problem because the technologies under consideration do not pose significant health hazards. The analysis of the panel and the results of the workshop indicate that the problem may be dealt with effectively through good communications and public education efforts. Privacy concerns about displaying images of bodies and initiating physical contact may prove to be significant hurdles to implementation. Several procedural steps are available to help alleviate these concerns. Convenience in the form of avoiding time delays appears to be a highly important factor in public acceptance, as well as in the overall successful functioning of the system. Technologies that take more than six seconds to screen each person are likely to encounter significant public resistance. It will be important to assess public reaction to, and acceptance of, the screening technologies. Methodological problems, which are inherent in carrying out such assessments, need to be taken into consideration to avoid obtaining invalid results.

9

Conclusions and Recommendations

Ensuring the security of the U.S. air travel system and of American and foreign air carriers traveling to and from the United States is a monumental task. Currently, in the United States, this involves screening over 1.5 million passengers and their carry-on baggage every day for the presence of metallic weapons or dangerous materials. The FAA is investigating and considering the implementation of new technologies that improve the effectiveness of current screening procedures by tailoring them to address and comply with current security requirements. At the same time, the FAA is looking into technologies that address anticipated changes in security requirements by expanding on the ability to detect the presence of dangerous materials on a person. After reviewing and assessing these efforts, the Panel on Passenger Screening reached the following conclusions.

ASSESSMENT OF SYSTEM ENHANCEMENTS

People relate the level of inconvenience and the invasion of privacy they are willing to tolerate to their perception of the severity of the threat being averted and the effectiveness of the screening efforts at averting that threat. For example, air carriers and passengers accept more intensive security procedures for international flights because they perceive a higher likelihood of terrorists targeting international flights. Passengers would probably resent intense screening measures for domestic U.S. travel unless they had proof that the severity of the threat was higher than usual. If the threat is high, more invasive technologies that may inconvenience passengers are likely to be more acceptable than when the threat is perceived to be low.

Because of the strong relationship between public acceptance of security-screening processes and the perception of risk, the panel believes the FAA should make this link explicit in a strategy for implementing new passenger screening technologies. Because it is impossible to predict the course that terrorists will take in the coming years, the FAA plan should include specific technologies that can be implemented in response to specific threats. The FAA should also examine how new technologies will be implemented over time in the absence of specific threats against U.S. air carriers or airports.

By openly addressing the link between the perceived level of threat and public acceptance of more intrusive security-screening processes, the FAA will help air carriers react more effectively to specific threats. Air carriers will also be able to plan the purchase of equipment based on new technologies as part of their regular efforts to upgrade security-screening equipment.

Although the panel can formulate some general conclusions and recommendations about new technologies for passenger screening, further efforts to assess public acceptance and to incorporate the resulting information into screening procedures will be needed to ensure the effective performance of individual technologies. Besides considering various public acceptance reactions to new screening technologies, the FAA will also have to determine an *acceptable* level of opposition. As discussed in chapter 1, a certain proportion of the public will oppose the implementation of any new technology. Therefore, the FAA will have to weigh the need for more effective airport security systems against the known opposition before mandating implementation of a new technology.

Assessing public acceptance of new screening systems and procedures is a relatively complex and difficult task. The degree to which people will accept the inconvenience, discomfort, delays, embarrassment, real or perceived health risks, and real or perceived invasion of privacy associated with passenger screening depends on the interaction of several variables. The most important variable is the perceived level of threat. The reactions of passengers, air carriers, and airport operators to any new screening technology will be strongly influenced by the perceived level of threat, and efforts to assess those reactions must take this effect into account.

Courts have generally interpreted current screening processes and technologies as a reasonable search under the administrative search exception to the Fourth Amendment, even though the search reveals personal information, in addition to the presence or absence of dangerous materials. New technologies probably will be considered in the same light, taking into account the degree of intrusiveness of the search procedure, the magnitude or frequency of the threat, and the sufficiency of alternatives. The courts will also consider the effectiveness of the search in reducing the threat and will determine whether sufficient care has been taken to limit the scope of the search as much as possible, without compromising effectiveness. Concerns will be raised about the legality of security screening or searches conducted without particularized probable cause, and new screening technologies are not likely to allay concerns about government surveillance of innocent people boarding an airplane.

The panel makes the following specific recommendations for using new technologies to improve passenger screening:

Recommendation: Indicate how new passenger screening technologies are integrated into long-range implementation plans for upgrading airport security.

Recommendation: Use a variety of means to assess public reaction to new passenger screening technologies:

- Identify important public acceptance issues by identifying similar or analogous circumstances from the past and by studying available information on public reaction to, and acceptance of, these circumstances.
- Assess public perception as early as possible in the development cycle.
- Assess public reactions to prototype systems.
- From earlier assessments, develop and maintain educational programs to inform the public about the advantages and perceived disadvantages of screening technologies.

Recommendation: Emphasize the importance of providing operators with information about the specific type and location of a threat item:

- *Convenience.* Screeners can more quickly determine whether or not the item that caused alarm is a threat, and passengers will experience less delay.
- *Privacy.* By allowing the screener to search only the area known to contain a suspect item, the screener is less likely to encounter external medical devices or other nonthreat objects that passengers consider personal.
- *Legality.* Limiting the search area will minimize the amount of information about nonthreat items passengers carry in their pockets and lessen the need for a policy on the discovery of illegal but nonthreat items. Current airport passenger screening techniques are open to charges that screeners may go beyond the limited right to search for threat objects. Technologies that allow only the identification of items considered a threat to the safety of the airport and the aircraft will eliminate this subtle element of doubt in the airport screening process. Air carriers and contract security companies must also ensure that their equipment is not designed or modified to detect materials that are not considered threat items.

IMPROVEMENTS TO CURRENT SCREENING SYSTEMS

Improvements to current metal-detector portal technology are expected to be transparent to passengers and the security-screening personnel. However, these improvements may increase screening efficiency by decreasing the number of false alarms and by allowing the screening personnel to resolve these alarms more quickly by providing information about the specific type and location of the object that triggered the alarm. Although no epidemiological studies have been conducted to evaluate the health effects of portal metal detectors and other passenger screening devices, data from epidemiological studies involving comparable radiation and field exposures from other sources suggest that there are no measurable health risks from these devices.

Although these technologies are mature and ubiquitous, the panel believes that improvements can be made to make them more effective for aviation security. The panel urges the FAA to continue to study technical ways to improve the metal-detection portals. Examples of areas where improvements can enhance the overall performance of current metal-detection portals are: (1) parallel algorithms for the simultaneous detection of different metals, alloys, and structures, and (2) detector arrays to localize contraband items within the portal.

TECHNOLOGIES TO MEET FUTURE PASSENGER SCREENING REQUIREMENTS

Technologies being developed can be broadly characterized as imaging technologies or trace-detection technologies.

Imaging Technologies

It is not necessary that imaging technologies produce *true-to-life* images of the person being screened. Images produced using a variety of methods, both passive and active, can be effectively interpreted by well trained screeners with sufficient experience. In the current state of technology development, operators are required to interpret the images because humans are familiar with the human form and its many variations. Several public acceptance issues regarding the display of *true-to-life* images are likely to make these technologies difficult to deploy as primary screening technologies in airports. The panel recommends some strategies to encourage the traveling public to accept the use of imaging technologies in their current state of development:

- Make sure the images are viewed by a person the same sex as the passenger.

- The displayed images should not be visible to anyone but screening personnel.
- Offer alternative screening procedures for people who object to imaging.
- Mask portions of the displayed image.
- Guarantee that the images will not be preserved beyond the brief screening procedure, except when questionable objects are detected.

The first three strategies will require large investments from air carriers and airports. These increases in costs have led the panel to conclude that these imaging technologies, as they exist today, are not suitable as primary screening procedures, that is, screening procedures to which every passenger must be subjected. There may be a place in the system for these technologies, as second or third screening alternatives; for example, after a passenger has been identified as posing a high risk, either through passenger profiling or through another screening technology. Specific recommendations to enhance the feasibility of implementing imaging technologies are as follows:

Recommendation: Determine how much distortion can be introduced into a human image before screeners lose the ability to detect threat objects.

Recommendation: Develop image-analysis routines to remove the screener from the primary inspection process.

Recommendation: Determine the time required for passenger screening under realistic airport screening conditions.

Recommendation: Develop an appropriate public education campaign on the levels of radiation exposure from imaging technologies, including specific information on comparative levels of radiation, and address specific concerns, such as the effects of radiation doses on pregnant women and on medical devices.

Recommendation: Quantify the threat level at which these imaging technologies would be acceptable for general screening.

Trace-Detection Technologies

Trace-detection technologies rely on the collection of samples of explosive materials to identify the presence of a threat material. Collection can entail sampling the air around a person or touching a person to remove particles of explosive materials from their person, clothing, or belongings.

Technologies that require touching a person to collect a sample raise the concern that people may not want to be touched, either by inanimate objects such as fronds or by people wielding hand-wand devices. This concern is difficult to address because the desire to maintain distance from strangers is a deeply ingrained response that is often influenced by basic cultural and religious beliefs. The *optimum* distance people maintain between themselves and other people varies greatly from person to person and from culture to culture and is not likely to be swayed by public information campaigns. Privacy concerns about initiating physical contact may prove to be a significant hurdle to implementation. Noncontact methods of sample collection, such as using an air shower or a vacuum, are likely to be more acceptable to passengers, but they are also likely to be less effective than contact sampling. Screening personnel may already feel intimidated by the people they are required to screen. Technologies that require even closer interaction between them and the passengers are likely to exacerbate this problem. A specific recommendation regarding new trace-detection technologies is:

Recommendation: For contact methods of sample collection, emphasize techniques that collect *secondary* samples from something a person has touched or techniques that involve collecting samples from a less personal area of the body, such as the hands.

Nonimaging Electromagnetic Technologies

The dielectric portal technology uses microwave energy to interrogate a passenger to detect the presence of metallic or nonmetallic objects. Like active imaging technologies, dielectric portal technology is likely to raise concerns about the use of radiation. However, if this technology can be made specific to threat objects, then it may improve the detection of nonmetallic objects without raising concerns about image projection and without requiring that an operator interpret the image.

OPERATOR PERFORMANCE

After investigating new technologies for screening passengers in airports, the panel determined that the systems presently used nationwide could be more effective by integrating the human operator more fully into the security system. The inability to maintain a high level of operator performance is a principal weakness of existing passenger screening systems and a potential weakness of future systems. Improving operator performance is as critical as technical improvements for enhancing current systems and ensuring the success of new passenger screening systems. Improving current technologies and developing new technologies both require balancing technological development and human operators in the overall security system.

Specific recommendations for improving operator performance in security-screening systems follow:

Recommendation: Develop techniques to measure operator performance for operators of current screening systems.

Recommendation: Study operator ergonomics, selection, training, and motivation for operators of current screening systems.

Recommendation: Determine the optimal balance between the automated system and the human operator in new systems.

References

American Cancer Society. 1995. Cancer Facts and Figures—1995. Atlanta, Georgia: American Cancer Society, Inc.

American Heart Association. 1995. Heart and Stroke Facts: 1995 Statistical Supplement. Dallas, Texas: American Heart Association.

AS&E (American Science and Engineering, Inc.). 1995. AS&E BodySearch™. Billerica, Massachusetts: American Science and Engineering.

ATA (Air Transport Association). n.d. Report of ATA Director of Security Harry J. Murphy. Washington, D.C.: Air Transport Association.

ATA (Air Transport Association). 1984. ATA Discussion Paper. Washington, D.C.: Air Transport Association. September 21, 1984.

ATA (Air Transport Association). 1994. Air Transport Association Annual Report of the U.S. Scheduled Airline Industry.

Ayres, B.D., Jr. 1994. For judge, a case where circumstances outweigh safeguards. The New York Times. July 8, 1994:A1.

Brent, R.L. 1980. Radiation teratogenesis. Teratology 21:281–298.

Browne, M.W. 1995. In search of security: radar scanners that undress people. The New York Times. May 5, 1995: A19.

Burnett, L., J. Pence, and H. Tramell. 1992. Technical evaluation of the Spatial Dynamics M600 Dielectrometer. Washington, D.C.: U.S. Customs Service.

14 C.F.R. (Code of Federal Regulations). 1995. §107.20.

Davies, D., and R. Parasuraman. 1982. The Psychology of Vigilance. London: Academic Press.

Dennison, S. 1995. Personal communication to the Panel on Passenger Screening. Washington, D.C. June 2, 1995.

Doll, R., and R. Peto. 1981. The causes of cancer: quantitative estimates of avoidable risks of cancer in the United States today. Journal of the National Cancer Institute 66:1191–1308.

Duval, J. 1995. Personal communication to the Panel on Passenger Screening. Washington, D.C. June 2, 1995.

FAA (Federal Aviation Administration). 1975. FAA Annual Report. Washington, D.C.: Federal Aviation Administration. April 17, 1975.

FAA (Federal Aviation Administration). 1981. Semi-Annual Report to Congress on the Effectiveness of the Civil Aviation Security Program: January 1, 1979–June 30, 1981. Washington, D.C.: Federal Aviation Administration.

FAA (Federal Aviation Administration). 1993. Criminal Acts Against Civil Aviation. Washington, D.C.: Office of Civil Aviation Security, Federal Aviation Administration.

FAA (Federal Aviation Administration). 1995. Personal communication to the Committee on Commercial Aviation Security. (Classified)

Fenello, M.J. 1973. Individual rights v. skyjack deterrence: an airline man's view. Villanova Law Review 18:996–997.

Fobes, J. 1995. Presentation to the Panel on Passenger Screening. Atlantic City, New Jersey. November 16, 1995. (Classified)

Graser, A. 1995. Personal communication to the Panel on Passenger Screening. Washington, D.C. June 2, 1995.

Gurney, J.G., B.A. Mueller, S. Davis, S.M. Schwartz, R.G. Stevens, and K.J. Kopecky. 1996. Childhood brain tumor occurrence in relation to residential power line configurations, electric heating sources, and electric appliance use. American Journal of Epidemiology 143:120–128.

Guzzo, R.A. 1988. Productivity research: reviewing psychological and economic perspectives. In Campbell, J.P., and R.J. Campbell, eds. Productivity in Organizations. San Francisco, California: Jossey-Bass.

Guzzo, R.A., R.D. Jette, and R.A. Katzell. 1985. The effects of psychologically based intervention programs on worker productivity: a meta-analysis. Personnel Psychology 38:275–291.

Hardage, M.L., J.R. Marbach, and D.W. Winsor. 1985. The pacemaker patient in the therapeutic and diagnostic device environment. Pp. 857–873 in Barold, S.S., ed., Modern Cardiac Pacing. Mount Kisco, New York: Futura Publishing Company.

Hertzberg, F. 1968. One more time: how do you motivate employees? Harvard Business Review (January-February):53-62.

Heureman, J.F. 1994. Florida v. Bostick: abandonment of reason in Fourth Amendment reasonable person analysis. Northern Illinois Law Review (13):173–197.

IRT Corp. n.d. Secure 1000: Hands-Off Security Screening. IRT-B-UUU-0793. San Diego, California: Nicolet Imaging Systems, A ThermoSpectra Company.

Issachoff, D. 1995. Presentation to the Panel on Passenger Screening. Washington, D.C. June 1995.

Jankowski, P. 1995a. Trace Explosives Detection Portal Workshop: January 1995. DOT/FAA/CT-TN95/05. Washington, D.C.: Federal Aviation Administration.

Jankowski, P. 1995b. Presentation to the Panel on Passenger Screening. Atlantic City, New Jersey. February 8, 1995.

Kheifets, L.I., A.A. Afifi, P.A. Buffler, and Z.W. Zhang. 1995. Occupational electric and magnetic field exposure and brain cancer: a meta-analysis. Journal of Occupational and Environmental Medicine 37:1327–1341.

LaFave W.R. 1987. Search and seizure: a treatise on the Fourth Amendment. 2nd ed. St. Paul, Minn.: West Coast Publishing.

Lawler, E.E. 1971. Pay and Organizational Effectiveness: A Psychological View. New York: McGraw-Hill.

Lawler, E.E. 1981. Pay and Organizational Development. Reading, Massachusetts: Addison-Wesley.

Limmer, L. 1995. Personal communication to the Panel on Passenger Screening. Washington, D.C June 2, 1995.

McGinely, P.W., and S.F. Downs. 1972. Airport searches and seizures: a reasonable approach. Fordham Law Review 41:293–306.

Mackie, R. 1987. Vigilance research—are we ready for countermeasures? Human Factors 29(6):707–724.

Microwave Cooking Handbook. n.d. Clifton, Virginia: Virginia International Microwave Power Institute.

Millitech Corporation. 1995. Image produced by Millitech's Contraband Detection System. South Deerfield, Massachusetts: Millitech Corporation.

Mossman, K.L., and L.T. Hill. 1982. Radiation risks in pregnancy. Obstetrics and Gynecology 60:237–242.

National Council on Radiation Protection and Measurements (NCRP). 1987. Ionizing Radiation Exposure of the Population of the United States. NCRP Report No. 93. Bethesda, Maryland: NCRP.

National Radiological Protection Board (NRPB). 1992. Electromagnetic Fields and the Risk of Cancer. Documents of the NRPB 3(1).

Nester, E.W., C.E. Roberts, and M.T. Nester. 1995. Microbiology: A Human Perspective. Dubuque, Iowa: William. C. Brown Publishers.

Nicolet Imaging Systems. 1995. Images and photographs from the SECURE 1000. San Diego, California: Nicolet Imaging Systems, A ThermoSpectra Company.

NRC (National Research Council). 1990. Health Effects of Exposure to Low Levels of Ionizing Radiation: BEIR V. Committee on the Biological Effects of Ionizing Radiation Washington, D.C.: National Academy Press.

NRC (National Research Council). 1993. Detection of Explosives for Commercial Aviation Security. National Materials Advisory Board Report 471. Washington, D.C.: National Academy Press.

Oak Ridge Associated Universities (ORAU). 1992. Health Effects of Low–Frequency Electric and Magnetic Fields.

ORAU 92/F8. Springfield, Virginia: National Technical Information Service.

PCAST (President's Commission on Aviation Security and Terrorism). 1990. Report of the President's Commission on Aviation Security and Terrorism.

Phillips, D. 1995. Airport security to be tightened. The Washington Post. August 9, 1995: A1.

Preston-Martin, S., W. Navidi, D. Thomas, P.J. Lee, J. Bowman, and J. Pogoda. 1996. Los Angeles study of residential magnetic fields and childhood brain tumors. American Journal of Epidemiology 143:105–119.

Public Law 101-604. 1990. Aviation Security Improvement Act of 1990.

Rasmussen, J. 1986. Information Processing and Human-Machine Interaction: An Approach to Cognitive Engineering. New York: North-Holland.

Reason, J. 1990. Human Error. Cambridge, Massachusetts: Cambridge University Press.

Smith, S.W. 1995. Hands-Off Security Screening with the Secure 1000 Nonintrusive Personnel Scanner. Nicolet Imaging Systems. Brochure provided to the Panel on Passenger Screening. October 1995.

United Nations Scientific Committee on Effects of Atomic Radiation (UNSCEAR). 1994. Sources and effects of ionizing radiation. New York: United Nations.

U.S. Bureau of the Census. 1994. Statistical Abstract of the United States: 1994. 114th ed. Washington, D.C.: U.S. Government Printing Office.

Welna, J. 1995. Personal communication to the Panel on Passenger Screening. Washington, D.C. June 2, 1995.

Wertheimer, N., and E. Leeper. 1979. Electric wiring configurations and childhood cancer. American Journal of Epidemiology 109:273–284.

Wiener, E.L. 1987. Cockpit automation. Pp. 433–461 in Wiener, E.L., and D.C. Nagel, eds., Human Factors in Aviation. San Diego, California: Academic Press.

CASE LAW REFERENCES

Bivens v. Six Unknown Named Agents of the Federal Bureau of Narcotics, 403 U.S. 388 (1971).

Camara v. Municipal Court, 387 U.S. 523, 537 (1967).

Carley v. Wheeled Coach, 991 F.2d 1117 (3rd Cir. 1993).

Carter v. Innisfree Hotel, No. 1940393, 1995 WL 277328 (Ala. May 12, 1995).

Cornfield v. Consolidated High School District, 230, 991 F.2d 1316 (7th Cir. 1993).

Covino v. Patrissi, 967 F.2d 73 (2nd Cir. 1992).

Dow Chemical Company v. United States, 476 U.S. 227, 237-39 (1986).

Florida v. Jimeno, 500 U.S. 248 (1991).

Florida v. Bostick, 501 U.S. 429 (1991).

Harkey v. Abate, 346 N.W.2d 74 (Mich. App. 1984).

Hartke v. Federal Aviation Administration, 369 F.Supp. 741 (E.D.N.Y. 1973).

Horton v. California, 496 U.S. 128 (1990).

Katz v. United States, 389 U.S. 347, 357 (1967).

Klarfeld v. United States, 962 F.2d 866, 870 (1992).

Klopp v. Wackenhut Corp., 824 P.2d 293, 300 (N.M. 1992).

Lebron v. National Railroad Corp., 115 S. Ct. 961, 964 (1995).

McMorris v. Alioto, 567 F.2d 897, 900-901 (9th Cir. 1978).

Michigan Department of State Police v. Sitz, 496 U.S. 444 (1990).

Ninth Circuit U.S. Appellate Court Opinion. June 29, 1973.

People v. Heimel, 812 P.2d 1177 (Colo. 1991).

Public Law 101-64. 1990. Aviation Security Improvement Act of 1990.

Rest. 2d Torts §652B. 1977. Restatement (Second) of Torts §652B. Philadelphia, Pennsylvania. American Law Institute.

Reynard v. NEC Corp., 887 F.Supp 1500 (M.D. Fla. 1995).

San Diego Gas & Electric Co. v. Superior Court, 38 Cal. Rptr.2d 811 (1995).

Schneckloth v. Bustamonte, 412 U.S. 218 (1973).

Skinner v. Railway Labor Executives Association., 489 U.S. 602, 619 (1989).

State v. Baez, 530 So.2d 405 (Fla. App. 3 Dist. 1988).

State v. Mark Anthony D., 433 S.E.2d 41 (W.Va. 1993).

State v. Perez, 509 So.2d 1287 (Dist. Ct. App. Fla. 1987).

Terry v. Ohio, 392 U.S. 1 (1968).

United States Constitution, Amendment IV.

United States v. $124,570 U.S. Currency, 873 F.2d 1240, 1244-1245 (9th Cir. 1989).

United States v. Albarado, 495 F.2d 799 (2nd Cir. 1974).

United States v. Blake, 888 F.2d 795 (1989).

United States v. Dalpiaz, 414 F.2d 374 (6th Cir. 1974).

United States v. Davis, 482 F.2d 893, 910 (9th Cir. 1973).

United States v. Doe, 829 F.Supp 511, 514 (D. Puerto Rico 1993).

United States v. Epperson, 454 F.2d 769, 771 (4th Cir. 1972).

United States v. Lopez-Pages, 767 F.2d 776, 778 (11th Cir. 1985).

United States v. Martinez-Fuerte, 428 U.S. 543, 558 (1976).

United States v. Morgan, 774 F.2nd 1215 6th Cir. 1985.

United States v. Pulido-Baquerizo, 800 F.2d 899, 902 (9th Cir. 1986).

United States v. Ramsey, 431 U.S. 531 (1977).

United States v. Roman-Marcon, 832 F.Supp 24 (D. Puerto Rico 1993).

United States v. Ross, 32 F.3d 1411, 1413 (9th Cir. 1994).

United States v. Ruiz-Estrella, 481 F.2d 723 (2nd Cir. 1973).

United States v. Sarkissian, 841 F.2d 959 (9th Cir. 1988).

United States v. Skipwith, 482 F.2d 1272, 1275 (5th Cir., 1973).

United States v. Sokolow, 490 U.S. 1, 10 (1989).

United States v. Vigil, 989 F.2d 337, 338 (9th Cir. 1993), cert. denied, 114 S.Ct. 205 (1993).

Vernonia School District 47J v. Acton, 115 S.Ct. 2386, 2390 (1995), citing Griffin v. Wisconsin, 483 U.S. 868, 873 (1987).

Wagner v. Metro Nashville Airport Authority, 772 F.2d 227 (6th Cir. 1985).

Williams v. Ellington, 936 F.2d 881 (6th Cir. 1991).

APPENDICES

APPENDICES

Appendix A

Laws, Regulations, and Treaties

FEDERAL STATUTES AND REGULATIONS

Anti-hijacking or Air Transportation Security Act of 1974 (Public Law 93-366) August 5, 1974. This law provided the statutory basis for the December 5, 1972, rule and "as part of its obligation under this Act, the FAA began a research and development program that emphasized the development of devices to protect air travelers against acts of criminal violence and aircraft piracy." (NRC. 1993.)

International Security and Development Act of 1985 (Public Law 99-83). This act provides for Federal Air Marshals, expansion of FAA R&D, assessment of security at foreign airports, and approval of foreign air carrier security programs.

Aviation Security Improvement Act of 1990 (Public Law 101-604) dated November 16, 1990. This act has been described in the 1992 FAA Annual Report to Congress as "perhaps the most comprehensive, far-reaching legislative initiative designed to improve all aspects of aviation security. It mandates many regulatory actions affecting several agencies, requires new reports, creates new organizations and staffing requirements, and empowers the FAA to promote and strengthen aviation security through an expedited, more focused research and development (R&D) program."

INTERNATIONAL PROTOCOLS AND TREATIES

Hijacking and sabotage of air carriers are not unique to the United States. Incidents of this type have affected air carriers worldwide, and a number of cooperative efforts have been undertaken on the international level to recognize and develop cooperative agreements to assist in solving this vexing problem.

The Tokyo Convention of September 1963. This treaty recognizes the inviolability of a hijacked aircraft and passengers, regardless of where the aircraft may be forced to land. The treaty provides that, in the event of a hijacking, the country where the aircraft lands must permit the aircraft, passengers, crew, and cargo to proceed to its destination as soon as is practical.

The Hague Convention of December 1970. The primary provision requires that every signatory state in which a hijacker is located must either extradite the offender to the state whose aircraft he hijacked or prosecute the hijacker. Signatory states must also provide severe penalties for the criminal offense of hijacking.

The Montreal Convention of September 1971. This convention provides for the application of principles of The Hague Convention to all crimes committed on board commercial aircraft. Elements included are: (1) violence against individuals aboard an aircraft, (2) damage to or destruction of an aircraft, and (3) placing devices or substances on an aircraft that could damage or destroy the aircraft, and (4) other crimes. The Montreal Convention also requires that states take all practical measures to prevent the commission of these offenses.

The Montreal Protocol of 1988. This protocol provides procedures for dealing with acts of violence against civil aviation at airports and ticket offices. The agreement was initiated as a result of terrorist attacks against the Rome and Vienna airports in 1987.

The Bonn Agreement. Signed on July 17, 1978, by the leaders of Britain, Canada, France, West Germany, Italy, Japan and the United States, this agreement was described in *The Washington Post* (July 18, 1978) as follows: "The heads of state and government, concerned over terrorism and hostage taking, declare that their governments will intensify their common undertaking to fight international terrorism. In cases in which a country refuses to extradite or legally prosecute airplane hijackers and/or give back such airplanes, the heads of state and government are unanimously agreed through their governments to take immediate action to cease all flights to that country. At the same time, their governments will implement steps to ban incoming flights from that country as well as flights by airlines of that country flying from any other country."

United States/Cuba Hijacking Agreement 2/15/73. This agreement provided for hijackers to be "returned to the party of registry of the aircraft or vessel or be brought before the courts of the party whose territory he reached for trial." Other portions of the agreement provided for facilitating "without delay the continuation of the journey of the passengers and crew innocent of the hijacking." The treaty was renounced by Cuba on February 15, 1977, although the Cuban government appears to have followed the intent of the agreement to the present.

International Civil Aviation Organization (ICAO). ICAO was established in 1944 by the Chicago Convention on International Civil Aviation. Annex 17 to the Chicago Convention establishes international security standards and recommended practices and requires member states to establish civil aviation security programs.

Appendix B

Follow-up Information from Workshop Attendees

This appendix contains material received from workshop participants subsequent to the June 1995 workshop.

ALVY DODSON, AIRPORT LAW ENFORCEMENT AGENTS NETWORK

June 7, 1995

Thank you for allowing me to attend the panel discussion on passenger screening. I appreciated the opportunity to participate with such a distinguished panel of experts, and I found the discussion of potential screening technologies very enlightening. Per your request, please accept the following observations and comments:

- The public perception of increased health risks from exposure to radiation sources should be addressed in a forthright and generally understandable manner. This perception will also be shared by security company and airline employees exposed to the proposed equipment.
- The costs associated with the equipment and technologies being considered must be a *major factor* and every effort should be made to hold those costs to a minimum. Federal funding should be made available for the purchase of this new equipment.
- The size and subsequent space requirements of the proposed equipment will be a major concern to air carriers and airports.
- Statistically, over 95 percent of dangerous weapons discovered in the screening process occur in the x-ray examination of carry-on luggage. This fact does not, however, diminish the need to improve and enhance the capabilities of walkthrough magnetometers.
- The development of this new technology should take into account the human factors which must be factored into this equation. The competency level of security screening personnel and the ever present employee turnover rate require systems that are simple to operate and, as much as possible, automatic in terms of detection and alarm.
- The personal obtrusiveness of any technology must be reasonable based on the threat perception of the travelling public balanced with the actual threat dictated by the intelligence community.

Electromagnetic I and II technology appears very promising, but the revealing nature of the "picture" may well require a secluded or shielded viewing screen analysis by screening personnel. The ability to resolve an anomaly should not stop the on-going screening process while a resolution is determined. The ability to "print" the original image would be advantageous in case of the detection of a dangerous weapon or component.

- Although a minimal risk, public concerns regarding airborne and skin contact biohazards should be considered in the development of trace detection technology.

A closing comment, post investigative analysis of terrorist attacks against civil aviation reveal that those responsible do their homework prior to a mission. This homework includes a thorough, "scouting" of the airport/airline security systems which may impede that mission. The development of new technologies should take into consideration the historically correct fact that improvised explosive devices are the weapon of choice for terrorists and that the physical separation of bomb components would be considered by a terrorist in order to reduce the chance of detection. Methods to detect power sources, initiators and timing devices in addition to explosives should be included in the new technology.

Hopefully, the introduction of this new technology, whatever its final configuration, will greatly enhance the passenger screening system nationwide with ancillary enhancement of the weakest portion of our system . . . checked luggage.

SUSAN RORK, AIR TRANSPORT ASSOCIATION AND DEBORAH McELROY, REGIONAL AIRLINE ASSOCIATION

June 30, 1995

Thank you for the opportunity to participate in the National Research Council panel discussion regarding future generation passenger screening technologies which are currently in the research phase of development.

The Air Transport Association and the Regional Airline Association representing the U.S. major and regional passenger airlines, jointly submit the following comments and observations for consideration by the Committee on Commercial Aviation Security for report to the Federal Aviation Administration.

It certainly was an interesting discussion particularly the privacy issues raised by representative from the American Civil Liberties Union (ACLU). The potential use of millimeter wave technology will be determined by the extent of the penetration and it's effect on one's physical privacy. Such invasive technology must be designed to detect only items identified as a real threat to civil aviation. To what degree the public is willing to accept a graphic display of their body parts to detect a weapon or explosive device unless the threat can be substantiated warrants examination by the Committee.

The cost of any new technology , manpower and space modifications is the first and foremost concern of the airline industry. We emphatically believe that prior to requiring any new passenger screening technologies, the FAA must conduct an unbiased cost benefit analysis. We recommend the Committee include in their report a thorough analysis of the cost issue, bearing in mind that the airline industry purchases all passenger screening equipment, contracts the services for screening personnel and pays rent for airport space with no assistance from the U.S. government.

The potential for increased health risks from exposure to radiation must be simply explained to the travelling public and air carrier personnel who routinely under go passenger screening. The travelling public is not sophisticated enough to understand that film and portable computers can be safely x-rayed, thus resulting in numerous unnecessary physical searches. Based on previous experience, it is reasonable to assume that employing radiation based technologies would necessitate more private screening, thus delaying the screening process.

The report should address the time needed for passenger processing and analysis and resolution of images by an operator. A well designed passenger screening checkpoint should be capable of processing a passenger through a walk through detector in the same amount of time it takes to clear their carry-on luggage through an x-ray machine.

The air carriers are opposed to any technology which would require more manpower than is currently required at a checkpoint or any restrictions to our current staffing flexibility. Electromagnetic technology must project on the viewing screening an androgynous image so the analysis can be accomplished by a male or female screener.

Any new technology development should include an analysis of the human factors associated with the training and operation of the technology. It is important to note that security screening companies have a fairly high employee turnover rate, and most screeners have very little education above the high school level. Image interpretation must be simple and procedures for resolving alarms must not be complicated.

The airline industry supports all efforts to improve security screening process and recognize our role to insure the security of our passengers, and aircraft. We appreciate the opportunity to comment and wish the committee success in their endeavor.

Sincerely,
(signed)
Susan 0. Rork
Managing Director Security

(signed)
Deborah McElroy
Vice President
Regional Airline Association
Air Transport Association

MEG LEITH, ASSOCIATION OF FLIGHT ATTENDANTS

June 30, 1995

AFA's primary focus revolves around the continued health and safety of our flight attendants. We do not wish to place any flight attendants at greater risk than necessary. As a consequence, our major concerns regarding these technologies are: 1) the risk of increased radiation exposure from improved imaging techniques and 2) protection for pregnant flight attendants from intrusive body contact and an increased level of radiation exposure. However, the lively discussion at the passenger screening meeting laid most of our fears to rest. These are our thoughts, as requested, regarding the potential passenger screening technologies as presented.

A. ELECTROMAGNETIC I

Since this technique is essentially the same as the electromagnetic portal method currently in effect and is not expected to impact the travelling public, AFA foresees no problems with planned improvements.

B. ELECTROMAGNETIC II

This technique is extremely invasive in terms of privacy. Examples of the projected images of the screened subjects show naked physiques in great detail, including revealing images of genital areas. If this method were to be instituted on a regular basis, very strict monitoring controls would be necessary. These images would have to be observed in an enclosed area to insure an individuals privacy and protect their modesty. Only persons of the same sex as the individuals being screened should monitor these images. This would require separate screening lines for male and female passengers.

If this screening technique were only to be implemented at times when a significant Level 2 threat exists (as identified in the chart provided in Attachment A), AFA feels that flight attendants would be much more understanding and accepting of this level of screening, even without the privacy protections listed above. An example of this level of threat would be the June 1995 Unabomber threat to aircraft departing from Los Angeles International Airport.

C. TRACE DETECTION

AFA does not think that any of the techniques that were displayed present a problem to passengers or flight attendants passing through them. However, the turnstile arms must move freely (without much pressure exerted by the individual passing through) to protect pregnant travellers.

D. WANDING

Since this technique remains the back-up method to screen individuals who may have tripped off an alarm or for those who cannot or chose not to go through the regular electromagnetic portal screening process, AFA does not foresee any problems with the continued use of this method of screening. If the trace detection function is integrated into the hand wand search devices, it will not alter the process in any substantive way; consequently, we do not have any objections to this method.

Appendix C

Selected Legal Cases Relevant to Aviation Security

Klarfeld v. United States, 962 F.2d 866, 870 (1992): claim for injunctive relief for a Constitutional violation, seeking to ensure that the security procedures at the Los Angeles Courthouse were not enforced in a manner that violated the Fourth Amendment.

Hartke v. Federal Aviation Admin., 369 F.Supp. 741 (E.D.N.Y. 1973): claim alleging a violation of Article I §6 of the U.S. Constitution; U.S. Senator sought to have search declared unconstitutional, as applied to him, FAA regulations pertaining to airport searches, as Article I §6 provides that Senators are privileged from seizures en route to Congress.

Wagner v. Metro Nashville Airport Authority, 772 F.2d 227 (6th Cir. 1985): claim under 42 U.S.C. §1983 seeking money damages for a state violation of federal civil rights; affirming summary judgment against plaintiff after finding no state action.

Bivens v. Six Unknown Named Agents of Federal Bureau of Narcotics, 403 U.S. 388 (1971): alleging federal violation of federal civil rights.

Dow Chemical Co. v. United States, 476 U.S. 227, 237–239 (1986): aerial photography of a chemical plant to detect possible violations of Clean Air Act does not constitute a search when no effort is made to protect against aerial surveillance.

Lebron v. Nat. Railroad Corp., 115 S.Ct. 961, 964 (1995): no constitutional problems without government action.

Vernonia School District 47J v. Acton, 115 S.Ct. 2386, 2390 (1995): upholding drug testing in schools; also noting the importance that the search was limited to student athletes where the risk of physical harm is particularly high; also, "the Fourth Amendment does not require that the least intrusive search be conducted"; at 2392: "by choosing to go out for the team [school athletes] voluntarily subject themselves to a degree of review even higher than that imposed on students generally."

Michigan Dept. State Police v. Sitz, 496 U.S. 444 (1990): allowing checkpoints for detecting drunk driving.

United States v. Martinez-Fuerte, 428 U.S. 543, 558 (1976): allowing checkpoint for detecting aliens.

United States v. Pulido-Baquerizo, 800 F.2d 899, 902 (9th Cir. 1986): stating "a visual inspection and limited hand search. . . . is a privacy invasion we believe free society is willing to tolerate."

United States v. Epperson, 454 F.2d 769, 771 (4th Cir. 1972): stating "the search for the sole purpose of discovering weapons and preventing air piracy. . . fully justified the minimal invasion of personal privacy by magnetometer."

United States v. Davis, 482 F.2d 893, 910 (9th Cir. 1973): stating "the potential damage to persons and property from [hijacking] is enormous. The disruption of air traffic is severe."

State v. Mark Anthony D., 433 S.E.2d 41 (W.Va. 1993): allowing strip searches only in exigent circumstances.

United States v. Epperson, 454 F.2d 769 (4th Cir. 1972): finding sufficient suspicion from the well known general danger.

LaFave (1987) at §10.6(c): noting that it is not clear that the 1972 profile system failed even once, thus undermining the basis for switching to a universal application search.

14 C.F.R. §108.17(e) (1995): requiring notification "posted in a conspicuous place at the screening station and on the x-ray system which notifies passengers . . . that [they are] being inspected."

Davis, at 912; *contra* LaFave, at §10.6(g): arguing that this offends common sense; if mere knowledge were sufficient to constitute consent, the government could subject anyone to a search notwithstanding the need, and the subject would be deemed to have consented.

United States v. Blake, 888 F.2d 795 (1989): consent to body search does not include groin area.

United States v. Sarkissian, 841 F.2d 959 (9th Cir. 1988): Federal Bureau of Investigation had limited time to intercept debarking Armenian terrorist on his way to a bombing.

N.Y. Times, July 8, 1994, at A1: Los Angeles police, after the murder of the ex-wife of O.J. Simpson and after seeing bloodstains on a van parked outside his estate, feared someone inside might be in danger.

Klopp v. Wackenhut Corp., 824 P.2d 293, 300 (N.M. 1992): Wackenhut not responsible for Klopp's tripping over stanchion base of metal detector when it had no authority to reposition it.

San Diego Gas & Electric Co. v. Superior Court, 38 Cal. Rptr.2d 811 (1995): plaintiffs unable to prove injury from electric and magnetic fields from power lines near their home.

Reynard v. NEC Corp., 887 F.Supp 1500 (M.D. Fla. 1995): plaintiff unable to prove brain tumor promoted by use of cellular telephone.

Carter v. Innisfree Hotel, No. 1940393, 1995 WL 277328 (Ala. May 12, 1995): allowing claim against hotel in which plaintiffs found evidence of a peeping tom.

Harkey v. Abate, 346 N.W.2d 74 (Mich. App. 1984): allowing claim against roller skating rink that placed hidden cameras in women's restroom.

THEORY AND PRACTICE OF SELECTED LEGAL ISSUES

Search or Seizure

The test for determining whether or not government observation constitutes a search is whether or not the defendant has a legitimate expectation of privacy in the place or thing searched (see *Terry v. Ohio*, 392 U.S. 1, 9 [1968]). This test has been applied with the practical result that government observation that reveals information only about the illegal activity of a defendant is not a search. (See, for example, *United States v. Place*, 462 U.S. 696, 707 [1983], holding that the warrantless use of a canine sniff did not violate the Fourth Amendment because the canine sniff only disclosed the presence or absence of narcotics and not unlimited information about the items searched.) This result is premised on the principle that a defendant has no legitimate expectation of privacy for contraband. Therefore, if it is only the contraband that is searched, and not incidentally the defendant's pockets or briefcase, the Fourth Amendment simply does not apply.

In theory, higher technology should be able to obtain information with more precision, thus allowing government officials to protect public safety without being hampered by the Fourth Amendment. In fact, a recent example illustrates that this may be the case.

In recent years, drug enforcement agencies have used forward-looking infrared devices (FLIR) to establish evidence of indoor marijuana cultivation (see *United States v. Field*, 855 F.Supp. 1518, 1522 [W.D. Wis 1994]). FLIR detects differences in the surface temperature of targeted objects, and because indoor cultivation requires the use of high intensity growlights, the device is able to detect a large amount of relative heat radiated from those lamps (see Tracy M. White, *The Heat Is On: The Warrantless Use of Infrared Surveillance to Detect Indoor Marijuana Cultivation*, 27 Ariz. St. L.J. 295, 296 [1995]). The constitutionality of the warrantless use of the FLIR has been upheld in number of recent cases (*United States v. Pinson*, 24 F.3d 1056 [8th Cir. 1994], *cert. denied*, 115 S.Ct. 664 [1994]; *United States v. Robertson*, 39 F.3d 891 [8th Cir. 1994], *cert. denied*, 115 S.Ct. 1812 [1995]; *United States v. Domitrovich*, 852 F.Supp. 1460 [E.D. Wash. 1994], *aff'd on other grounds*, 1995 WL 358624 [9th Cir. June 15, 1995]; *United States v. Porco*, 842 F.Supp. 1393 [D. Wyo. 1994]; *United States v. Deaner*, 1992 WL 209966 [M.D. Pa. July 27, 1992], *aff'd on other grounds*,

1 F.3d 192 [1993]; *United States v. Penny-Feeney*, 773 F.Supp. 220 [D. Haw. 1991], *aff'd*, 984 F.2d 1053 [1991]; *United States v. Ford*, 34 F.3d 992 [11th Cir. 1994]; *State v. McKee*, 510 N.W.2d 807 [Wis. 1993]).

The Eighth Circuit has upheld the constitutionality of the use of the FLIR device by the Drug Enforcement Agency on the grounds that the defendant had no legitimate expectation of privacy in the heat emanating from his home, the only information obtained (*Pinson*, 24 F.3d 1056, 1058). The Eighth Circuit opted to use a two-pronged formulation of the legitimate expectation of privacy test. Under this test, a legitimate expectation of privacy exists only where "(1) the individual manifests a subjective expectation of privacy in the object of the challenged search; and (2) society is willing to recognize that subjective expectation as reasonable" (*Id.*, at 1058 [quoting *Katz v. United States*], 389 U.S. 347, 361 [1967] [Harlan J., concurring]). Applying this rule, the court concluded that even if Pinson had a subjective expectation of privacy in the heat emanating from his home, society was not willing to recognize that expectation as reasonable (*Id.*, at 1058).

The *Pinson* court analogized the use of FLIR to two other types of cases (*White*, at 297). First, the court looked to *California v. Greenwood*, where the Supreme Court found that persons cannot have a legitimate expectation of privacy in garbage bags left at the curb, because those bags "are readily accessible to animals, children, scavengers, snoops, and other members of the public" and are placed at the curb for the express purpose of having a third party remove the bags (486 U.S. 35, 40-41 [1988]). Second, and more importantly, the court compared the use of FLIR to the use of drug sniffing dogs (*Pinson*, at 1058).

In *United States v. Place*, the Supreme Court held that the warrantless use of a canine sniff did not violate the Fourth Amendment because the canine sniff disclosed only the presence or absence of narcotics and nothing more (462 U.S. 696, 707 [1983]). The *Place* court reasoned that the canine sniff was less intrusive than a typical search and that the limited disclosure exposed the property owner to a minimum amount of embarrassment and inconvenience compared to other investigative methods (*Id.*, at 707). The *Pinson* court analogized that because the sense-enhancing canine sniff could constitutionally detect odor escaping from a suitcase, the sense-enhancing infrared device could constitutionally detect heat escaping from a home (*Pinson*, at 1058). The *Pinson* court further reasoned that "none of the interests which form the basis for the need for the protection of a residence, namely the intimacy, personal autonomy, and privacy associated with a home, are threatened by thermal imagery" (*Id.*, at 1059). Nevertheless, other courts have found that these interests are threatened by thermal imagery (*United States v. Field*, 855 F.Supp. 1518 [W.D. Wis. 1994]; *United States v. Ishmael*, 843 F.Supp. 205 [E.D. Tex. 1994], *aff'd*, 48 F.3d 850 [5th Cir. 1995]; *State v. Young*, 867 P.2d 593 [Wash. 1994] [dicta]).

Therefore, these courts have found FLIRs to constitute a search under the Fourth Amendment.

The *Ishmael* court found the FLIR to constitute a search, because it was able to distinguish the FLIR from a canine sniff. First, the FLIR cannot distinguish between *contraband heat* and *legal heat*. Thus, the information revealed is more indiscriminate and more intrusive than a canine sniff (*Ishmael*, 843 F.Supp. 205, 213). Second, although a dog's sense of smell is more discerning than a human's, it does not parallel the use of an infrared device that can detect minute heat gradations from 1500 feet away (*Id*).

The first argument of the *Ishmael* court has been widely rejected because information gained from the surveillance does not reveal unlimited information, but only information restricted to one activity, heat generation (*Deaner*, 1992 WL 209996, at *4). The *Ishmael* court's second argument has also been widely rejected because although an infrared device is more sensitive than the olfactory sense of a dog, this fact alone does not make the comparison dissimilar. Both investigative methods involve sense-enhancing equipment to find criminal evidence that is otherwise not detectable by human sense. The degree of undetectability should not be the standard for measuring whether an investigative method is appropriate (White, at 300).

The *Young* court found use of the FLIR to constitute a search because it reveals information not solely related to the presence of contraband. "The device allowed officers to draw specific inferences about the inside of the house . . . which particular rooms a homeowner is heating. . . . , the number of people who may be staying at the residence" (*Young*, 867 P.2d 593, 598). At least one court has held that it is dispositive that the officers did not "see" inside the house. Because the observation in question tangibly produced only heat patterns, any other information must be just inferences that might be drawn from the infrared results (*Domitrovitch*, 852 F.Supp. 1460, 1474 [E.D. Wash. 1994]). Nevertheless, by requiring actual sight to make an observation, a search seems to ignore the very nature of modern technology.

The Ninth Circuit has remanded a case for more explicit findings on the technological capabilities of FLIR (*United States v. Kyllo*, 37 F.3d 526 [9th Cir. 1994]). Notably, the court stated that its analysis would be affected by "for example . . . whether this device can detect sexual activity in the bedroom . . . or at the other extreme, whether it can only detect hot spots where heat is escaping from a structure" (White, at 308 [quoting *Kyllo*, No. 93-30231, 1994 WL 259823, at *3]). In other words, although the information obtained through the use of FLIRs might be merely about heat patterns, in order to avoid probable cause and warrant requirements of the Fourth Amendment, the inferences that can be drawn from that information may have to be limited to that regarding illegal activity.

Ishmael, Young, and *Kyllo* seem to not bode well for other technology-based searches. First, high resolution radars, for example, can interpret the reflection of a high-energy pulse in the form of an image (see Lisa J. Steele, The view from on high: satellite remote sensing technology and the fourth amendment, High. Tech. L.J. 6:317,333 [1991]). No inference even needs to be made. The information itself is broader than that related to illegal activity. Second, even though these three courts are in the minority, it is important to note that FLIRs have only be used to observe houses.

The home is one of the places most deserving of protection from government intrusion (*Field*, 855 F.Supp 1518, 1519; compare *U.S. v. Knotts*, 460 U.S. 276, 285 [1983] [finding government use of an electronic beeper to track the movement of a vehicle did not constitute a search]) with *United States v. Karo*, 468 U.S. 705, 717 [1984] [finding that monitoring a beeper inside a residence did constitute a search]). Even canine sniffs constitute searches when done at a residence (*United States v. Thomas*, 757 F.2d 1359 [2d Cir. 1985], *cert. denied*, 474 U.S. 819 [1985]). Nevertheless, not even the home is as deserving of protection as a person's body (*Sepulvida v. Ramirez*, 967 F.2d 1413 [9th Cir. 1992], *cert. denied*, 114 S.Ct. 342 [1993]; *York v. Story*, 324 F.2d 450, 454 [9th Cir. 1963] ["we cannot conceive of a more basic subject of privacy than the naked body"], *cert. denied*, 376 U.S. 939 [1964]). For this reason even relatively unintrusive searches of an individual's person have been held to constitute searches.

The magnetometer, though minimally intrusive has been found to constitute a search within the meaning of the Fourth Amendment (*United States v. Epperson*, 454 F.2d 769 [4th Cir. 1972], *cert. denied*, 406 U.S. 947 [1972]). The x-ray scanner, certainly a more intrusive device than a magnetometer, has also been found to constitute a search (*United States v. Henry*, 615 F.2d 1223 [9th Cir. 1980]; *contra Shapiro v. State*, 390 So.2d 344 [Fla. 1982], *cert. denied*, 450 U.S. 982 [1982]). Pulsed radar scanners, which produce an image of an individual's naked body, are clearly the most intrusive of all security searching devices. Nevertheless, "with the Supreme Court's recent laissez faire attitude toward law enforcement searches and seizures," the list of surveillance devices that fall outside the scope of the Fourth Amendment may well be extended (see Brian J. Serr, Great expectations of privacy: a new model for fourth amendment protection, Minn. L. Rev., 73:583, 585; 1989; *see also State v. Cannon*, 634 S.W.2d 648 [Tenn. Ct. App. 1982] [use of a nightscope does not constitute a search]).

The old rule to determine what is and is not a search required a physical intrusion. This test was insufficient, however, to protect against invasions like wiretapping where no physical intrusion was made. The new rule, by not requiring a physical intrusion, seemed to give broader protection. Under the new rule, government conduct would constitute a search whenever it physically or otherwise invades an area in which the individual has a legitimate expectation of privacy (*Rakas v. Illinois*, 439 U.S. 128, 143–144 [1978]). Unfortunately, this rule is more amenable to interpretation than the old rule.

Although there is little question whether the presence of police officers in your home constitutes a physical intrusion, there can be a big question whether your expectation of privacy in your bank records is *legitimate.* By mere participation in modern life, individuals surrender much information about themselves. What this has often meant in terms of the Fourth Amendment is that any expectations of privacy in these matters is, since they have already been exposed to some degree, no longer legitimate (see Lewis R. Katz, In search of a Fourth Amendment for the 21st century, Ind. L.J. 65:549, 563–575; 1987). The problem is that as technology advances it becomes easier to characterize information as *exposed,* because it is at all possible to detect it (Daniel J. Polatsek, Thermal imaging and the Fourth Amendment: pushing the Katz test toward terminal velocity, J. Computer & Information L. 13:453, 476–479; 1995).

The Department of Justice seems to be counting on this sort of judicial response. Through the National Institute of Justice, the department is developing its own technology to address Fourth Amendment requirements (David Van Biema, Peekaboo: the new detector [Time, Mar. 27, 1995:29]). With the relaxation of concealed-weapons laws, the need to identify individuals armed with illegal weapons has grown dramatically. Yet, the Fourth Amendment prohibits frisking someone without reasonable suspicion. If technology could pinpoint a weapon at a distance of 12 feet without an invasive search, it might justify subsequent frisks and confiscation.

In any case, "it is doubtful that [airline] passengers today have [a reasonable expectation of privacy with regard to the intrusion]" (Lenett, at 564). The frequency of the intrusion argument failed 20 years ago (*United States v. Davis,* 482 F.2d 893, 905 [9th Cir. 1973]). Yet, "until only a few years ago . . . metal detectors were used primarily at airports, political conventions, the Olympics, and some rap shows. Now they're standard equipment at nightclubs, card clubs, schools, and almost all major concerts" (Deborah Sullivan, Metal detector sales rise with crime, L.A. Times [June 30, 1994:8]). By systematic practice, expectations of passengers have been reconditioned. Nevertheless, expecting to be searched at all is one thing. Expecting to be searched in a very intrusive manner is quite another.

Although people are searched more often nowadays, it is not at all clear that they are being searched in a more intrusive manner. Persons can have more of an expectation of privacy in a radar reflection pattern than in the heat escaping from one's home. Even if expectations not to be searched at all are no longer legitimate, there is no corresponding reason why expectations not to be searched in an intrusive manner are not still legitimate.

Government Conduct

If the first threshold element is satisfied and there is a search, then the next threshold element that must be satisfied

for the Fourth Amendment to be applicable is that the search has been performed by the government. Private conduct, even if wrongful, is not subject to the Fourth Amendment (see *Jackson v. Metropolitan Edison,* 419 U.S. 345, 349 [1974]). Therefore, it is important to determine whether private airlines act as government "agents" when they search and screen passengers pursuant to a federal regulation.

The FAA requires airline to institute security procedures to screen passengers (14 C.F.R. §108). In the Ninth Circuit it has long been established that "the government's involvement in promulgating the FAA guidelines to combat hijacking is so pervasive as to bring any search conducted pursuant to that program within the reach of the Fourth Amendment" (*United States v. Ross,* 32 F.3d 1411, 1413 [9th Cir. 1994] [quoting *United States v. Davis*], 482 F.2d 893, 904 [9th Cir. 1973]). Nevertheless, even the Ninth Circuit has found some airline searches to be private conduct, and thus not subject to the *reasonableness* requirement of the Fourth Amendment. Such a finding is made when the court determines that the search was clearly not pursuant to the FAA regulations (*United States v. Pierce,* 893 F.2d 669 [5th Cir. 1990], *cert. denied,* 113 S.Ct. 621 [1992]; *United States v. Gumerlock,* 590 F.2d 794 [9th Cir. 1979] [airport shipment which was not subject to airport mandatory screening procedures was a private one], *cert. denied,* 441 U.S. 948 [1979]).

The Ninth Circuit approach is shared by the Eighth (*United States v. Echols,* 477 F.2d 37 [8th Cir. 1973] [holding that search is not government action when not done pursuant to FAA regulations], *cert. denied,* 414 U.S. 825 [1973]). Yet other circuits still find that airline searches, even when conducted pursuant to FAA regulations, constitute private conduct (see, for example,. *United States v. Morgan,* 774 F.2d 1215 [6th Cir. 1985]; *United States v. Kevlian,* 602 F.2d 1033 [2d Cir. 1979]).

The Supreme Court has not addressed the specific issue of whether airport security searches constitute government action. Yet, an important group of cases, *Jackson v. Metropolitan Edison,* 419 U.S. 345 (1974), *Blum v. Yaretsky,* 457 U.S. 991 (1982), and *Rendell-Baker v. Kohn,* 457 U.S. 830 (1982), stands for the principle that "unless the government affirmatively influences or coerces the private party to undertake the challenged action, such conduct is not state action for constitutional purposes" (*Lebron v. Nat. Railroad Corp.,* 115 S.Ct. 961, 980 [1995] [O'Connor J., dissenting]; the majority of the court did find Amtrak to be a government actor by virtue of the structure of Amtrak).

An application of this test to the airport security search leaves no doubt that security searches constitute state action; 14 C.F.R. §108 not just encourages but mandates that all airlines implement security programs (14 C.F.R. §§108.5-108.13). These regulations are so detailed that they even describe employment standards for screening personnel (14 C.F.R. §108.31). The FAA can be though of as *responsible* for the searches (*Blum v. Yaretsky,* 457 U.S. 991, 1005

[1982]). In contrast, the court found in *Blum* that decisions made by a hospital to discharge patients were not state action despite the fact that Medicaid regulations may have prompted those decisions. The actions in *Blum* turned ultimately on medical judgments made by private parties according to professional standards not established by the state (*Id*). In contrast, the FAA has not just mandated that searches be made, but has specified just how they must be made. It seems that the second threshold requirement of the Fourth Amendment is met. This means that airport security searches are subject to the Fourth Amendment. By no means do these searches necessarily violate the Fourth Amendment. This screening seems to fit into several Fourth Amendment exceptions.

KLARFELD V. UNITED STATES

Myron Klarfeld, an attorney, entered the U.S. Courthouse in Los Angeles and, even after removing all metal objects and his jacket, twice set off the magnetometer alarm (*Klarfeld v. United States*, 944 F.2d 583, 585 [9th Cir. 1991], *en banc denied*, 962 F.2d 866 [1992]). Klarfeld asked to be searched by the marshal's metal hand detector. However, the guard allegedly refused to do so and ordered Klarfeld to go back through the metal detector and remove his belt and shoes and place them on the metal detector (*Id*). Klarfeld argued that this was unnecessarily intrusive, since a hand-held magnetometer was available and would have enabled the marshals to determine whether he was carrying a weapon without removing his shoes. All three judges reversed a dismissal of Klarfeld's claim. One judge agreed not only with Klarfeld's main argument, but also with his argument that California lawyers have as extensive background checks as court personnel who do not get screened (*Id.*, at 588 [Pregerson, J concurring]; but see *Klarfeld*, 962 F.2d 866, 869 [1992] [Kozinski, J., dissenting] ["screening is always intrusive . . . there is no constitutional right to choose the particular screening method . . . to be subjected to"]).

UNITED STATES V. $124,570 U.S. CURRENCY

The court in *United States v. $124,570 U.S. Currency* found the search in that case not to be conducted pursuant to the narrow objective of ensuring airline and airport safety.

In *$124,570 U.S. Currency*, Flight Terminal Security (FTS) at Seattle International Airport noticed a dark mass in the briefcase of Wayne Campbell. Campbell, although initially reluctant, eventually permitted an FTS. officer to search the case behind a private screen (*$124,570 U.S. Currency*, 873 F.2d 1240, 1241). The officer discovered the large amount of cash, questioned Campbell as to his destination, and released him. The officer reported the discovery of Campbell's cash to the U.S. Customs Service. FTS officers are paid $250 for each report of sums of currency in excess of $10,000. Based on this report, Customs and Drug Enforcement Agency agents met Campbell when he arrived at Los Angeles International Airport and seized the money.

The Ninth Circuit noted the emphasis of the Supreme Court on the importance of keeping administrative searches free of the government's separate motive of criminal investigation (*Id.* at 1244 [relying upon *Camara v. Municipal Court*], 387 U.S. 523 [1967]). The court found that the close working relationship between the FTS and the local law enforcement at Seattle airport, along with monetary rewards, was likely to affect the actions of FTS agents in prohibited ways (*cf. Dolan v. Continental Airlines*, 526 N.W.2d 922 [Mich. App. 1995] [airline concerned about overzealous reporting fired ticket agent who did not follow internal reporting procedures]; compare *United States v. Canada*, 527 F.2d 1374 [9th Cir. 1975] [upholding seizure where there was no evidence of a cooperative relationship of financial reward]. FTS officers can only open packages pursuant to the approved objective of ensuring air safety (*124,570 U.S. Currency*, 873 F.2d 1240, 1246). The FTS agent in *24,570 U.S. Currency* had no safety-related justification for further inquiry into Campbell's affairs after determining his briefcase contained no weapons of explosives (*Id*).

Appendix D

Biographical Sketches of Panel Members

George Swenson, Jr., is professor emeritus of electrical and computer engineering and of astronomy at the University of Illinois, Urbana. His fields of specialization are electromagnetic and acoustic wave phenomena and radio astronomy. Dr. Swenson has served as head of the Departments of Astronomy and of Electrical and Computer Engineering, director of the Vermilion River Observatory of that university, and chairman of the Very Large Array (VLA) conceptual design group at the National Radio Astronomy Observatory. He has served on numerous National Research Council committees during the past 40 years.

Homer Boynton has extensive experience in security matters, including 25 years with the Federal Bureau of Investigation and 12 years with American Airlines as managing director of corporate security. He has chaired many advisory panels on airline security, including the Security Advisory Committee of the Air Transport Association and the Security Committee of the International Air Transport Association. He was a member of the FAA Research, Engineering and Development Advisory Committee.

Barry D. Crane of the Institute for Defense Analysis has a broad background in developing test and evaluation procedures for military hardware. He received his B.S. degree in physics from the U. S. Air Force Academy, and his M.S. and Ph.D. degrees in physics from the University of Arizona. He was responsible for developing drug-detection technology for the director of defense research and engineering until 1991. He is currently evaluating detection and monitoring capabilities of U.S. government surveillance assets used to find and follow air and maritime drug traffickers. He is also responsible for evaluating tactical aircraft testing for the director of operational test and evaluation, Office of the Secretary of Defense.

Douglas H. Harris is chairman and principal scientist of Anacapa Sciences, Inc. He has training in psychology, engineering, statistics, and military science and a Ph.D. from Purdue University in 1959. He has 36 years of experience in the analysis of systems operations, the measurement of human performance, the design and evaluation of human/machine systems, and the development of training programs and performance aids. He is a fellow and a former president of the Human Factors and Ergonomics Society, and a past chair of the NRC Committee on Human Factors and the Panel on Organizational Linkages.

Wilfred A. (Bill) Jackson received his B.S. degree in business administration from West Virginia University and his M.S. degree in management from George Washington University. In 1974 he graduated from the Industrial College of the Armed Forces at Ft. McNair, Washington, D.C. He served with the U.S. army for 26 years before being employed by the BDM Corporation, Mitre Corporation, BWI Airport, and the Airport Operators Council International. He recently joined the University of North Dakota as assistant professor at the Center for Aerospace Sciences. Mr. Jackson is accredited by the American Association of Airport Executives.

Jiri (Art) Janata is associate director of the Environmental Molecular Science Laboratory at the Pacific Northwest National Laboratory. He received his Ph.D. in analytical chemistry from Charles University (Prague) in 1965 and was on the faculty at the University of Utah for 20 years. His current interests include interphasial chemistry, chemical sensors and electroanalytical chemistry with particular emphasis on environmental applications. Dr. Janata has authored more than 120 papers and has 15 U.S. patents.

Kenneth Laughery is the Herbert S. Autrey Professor of Psychology at Rice University. He has published extensively in the area of risk perception, particularly with respect to the risks involved in common daily activities, such as driving and swimming. He teaches courses in psychology and engineering psychology, as well as in several areas of human factors and system reliability and safety. He chaired the President's Forum at the Human Factors and Ergonomics Society meeting on Human Factors and the American Consumer and has been a panel participant at the same conference in other areas of ergonomics. Dr. Laughery is a former president of the Human Factors and Ergonomics Society. Within the past year he has given keynote addresses at international ergonomics meetings in Brazil and Australia.

Harry Martz is the nondestructive evaluation research and development thrust area leader for Lawrence Livermore National Laboratory. He received his B.S. degree in 1979 from Siena College and his M.S. and Ph.D. degrees in 1986 from

Florida State University. For six years he led the a project in applying computed tomography and x-ray and proton radiography to material characterization and gamma-ray gauge techniques to treaty verification activities. His current projects include the use of nonintrusive x- and gamma-ray computed tomography techniques as three-dimensional imaging tools to understand material properties and to assay radioactive waste forms.

Kenneth Mossman of the Department of Microbiology at Arizona State University has over 10 years experience in the effects of low-level ionizing radiation, especially in the areas of radiation risk assessment and risk perception. He has worked with the Commission on Life Sciences Board on Radiation Effects Research and is a member of the Committee for the Evaluation of the 1950's Air Force Human Testing in Alaska using Radioactive Iodine 131 (Commission on Geosciences, Environment and Resources, Polar Research Board). Dr. Mossman is a former president of the Health Physics Society.

Paul Rothstein is professor of law at the Georgetown University Law Center. He is a specialist in civil and criminal lawsuits and Supreme Court jurisprudence. He has been advisor to the Federal Judicial Center on Scientific Evidence, to the U.S. Congress (both the House of Representatives and Senate) on evidence and criminal law; to the National Conference of Commissioners on uniform state laws on uniform rules of evidence; and to a number of former Soviet countries on drafting new constitutions, individual rights, and establishing of a judiciary. He has been chairman of the American Bar Association Committee on Criminal Procedure and Evidence and chairman of the Association of American Law Schools Evidence Section, among others. Professor Rothstein received B.S. and J.D. degrees from Northwestern University. He received a Fullbright scholarship to Oxford University upon graduation from law school as first in the class and editor-in-chief of the law review. He has published four books and approximately 100 articles in the area of judicial processes.

1. Report No. DOT/FAA/AR-96/52	2. Government Accession No.	3. Recipient's Catalog No.
4. Title and Subtitle New Technologies for Airline Passenger Security Screening: Implementation Issues		5. Report Date June 1996
		6. Performing Organization Code
7. Author(s) Committee on Commercial Aviation Security Panel on Passenger Screening		8. Performing Organization Report No.
9. Performing Organization Name and Address National Materials Advisory Board National Research Council 2101 Constitution Avenue, NW Washington, Dc 20418		10. Work Unit No. (TRAIS)
		11. Contract or Grant No. DTFA03-94-C-00068
12. Sponsoring Agency Name and Address Federal Aviation Administration Technical Center Aviation Security Research and Development Service Atlantic City International Airport, NJ 08405		13. Type of Report and Period Covered Final Report
		14. Sponsoring Agency Code AAR-500

15. Supplementary Notes

The FAA's Contracting Officer's Technical Representatives (COTR) were Ronald Krauss and James Connelly.

16. Abstract

Issues regarding the implementation of automated systems being considered by the Federal Aviation Administration for screening airline passengers in airports are assessed in this report. In addition to metal-based eapons, the new technologies also can detect plastic explosives and other non-metallic weapons. Issues such as health risks, privacy, and traveler comfort are evaluated for each technology. Alternative screening methods for passengers who want to avoid an automated system also are suggested.

17. Key Words Passenger Screening Legal Concerns Imaging Technology Risk Assessment Trace Detection Technology Human Factors Health Concerns Privacy		18. Distribution Statement	
19. Security Classif. (of this report) Unclassified	20. Security Classif. (of this page) Unclassified	21. No. of Pages 86	22. Price

Form DOT F1700.7 (8–72)   Reproduction of completed page authorized